Via Cavour

Viale Giacomo Matteotti

Via Mascagno

Via Manelli

Viale dei Mille

Via Campo D'Arigo

Piazza Savonarola

English Church

Via P. A. Micheli

Via degli Artisti

Via de Della Robbio

Viale Manfredofanti

GIARDINO DEI SEMPLICI

Via Gino Capponi

GIARDINO DELLA GHERARDESCA

Piazzale Donatello

Via G. La Farina

Università

S. S. Annunziata

Borgo Pinti

Via Giuseppe Giusti

Via della Robbio

Benedeto

Varchi

Viale Giuseppe Mazzini

Via Campo D'Arigo

Pza. della S.S. Annunziata

Via della Colonna

Viale Antonio

Via della Robbio

Via Mascacio

Via Capo di Mondo

Alfani

Via della Colonna

Piazza M. D'Azeglio

Via G Bovio

Via Manelli

ria n Hospital

Borgo Pinti

S. Maria dei Pazzi

Gramsci

Via Capo di Mondo

Via Luca Landucci

Via dei Pilastri

Synagogue

Via della Mattonaia

Piazza Oberdan

riuolo

Pza G. Salvemini

S. Ambrogio

Via Pietro Colletta

Via Capo di Mondo

Borgo La Croc

Piazza Beccaria

Via Vincenzo Gioberti

Via Vincenzo Gioberti

Via Ghibellina

Via dell' Agnolo

Viale Giovanni Amendaola

Via Orcagna

Campofiore

Piazza S. Croce

Via Ghibellina

S. Croce

Via S. Giuseppe

Viale Giovine Italia

Via Fra' Giovanni Angelico

del

Plagentina

National Library

Via Tripoli

Piazza Piave

Via via

Lungarno della Vecchia

Via Orcagna

Fiume Arno

Lung. del Tempio

Serristori

Ponte San Niccolò

Lung. B. Cellini

Piazza F. Ferrucci

Lungarno Franceso Ferrucci

Piazzale Michelangelo

Via

Via d. Elia Canina

S. Salvatore al Monte

Viale Michelangelo

di

Coluccio

Salutati

Rusciano

Basilica S. Miniato al Monte

Viale Michelangelo

RICORBOLI

Florence

400 m / 0.25 miles

MONTE ALLE CROCI

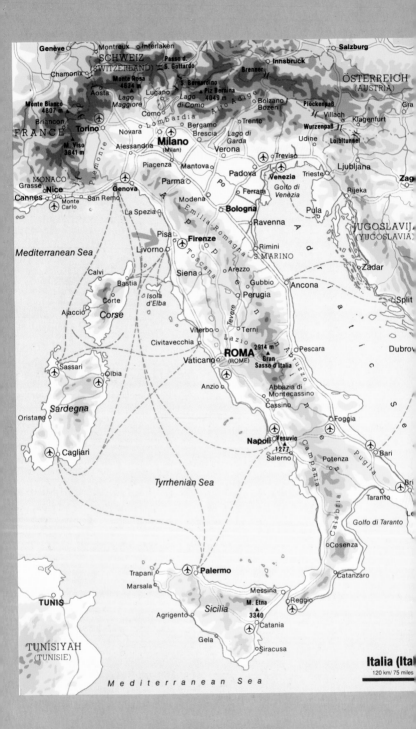

INSIGHT *Pocket* GUIDES

FLORENCE

Written and Presented by **Christopher Catling**

Christopher Catling

INSIGHT
Pocket
GUIDES

Insight Pocket Guide:

FLORENCE

Directed by
Hans Höfer

Managing Editor
Andrew Eames

Photography by
Robert Mort

Design Concept by
V. Barl

Design by
Carlotta Junger

© 1994 APA Publications (HK) Ltd

All Rights Reserved

Printed in Singapore by
Höfer Press (Pte) Ltd
Fax: 65-8616438

Distributed in the United States by
Houghton Mifflin Company
222 Berkeley Street
Boston, Massachusetts 02116-3764
ISBN: 0-395-68230-4

Distributed in Canada by
Thomas Allen & Son
390 Steelcase Road East
Markham, Ontario L3R 1G2
ISBN: 0-395-68230-4

Distributed in the UK & Ireland by
GeoCenter International UK Ltd
The Viables Center, Harrow Way
Basingstoke, Hampshire RG22 4BJ
ISBN: 9-62421-563-4

Worldwide distribution enquiries:
Höfer Communications Pte Ltd
38 Joo Koon Road
Singapore 2262
ISBN: 9-62421-563-4

Benvenuto!

Welcome! To me, Florence is not just a tourist destination, it is a city that can fundamentally change your life. I first went there while I was working in Tuscany as an archaeologist, at a time when my taste in art was aggressively pro-modern; arrogantly, I did not believe that anything painted before Van Gogh could hold any interest whatsoever for me, and especially not religious art. Florence taught me how wrong I could be.

Ever since, when writing about Florence, I have tried to provide a painless introduction to the city's complex history and its wealth of art and architecture, in the hope of persuading others to take the same journey as me — from relative ignorance to relative enlightenment. In this book I have arranged three day-long itineraries for you which cover the essential sights, such as the renowned Uffizi gallery, the Ponte Vecchio and the Pitti Palace. Furthermore, my range of optional tours will take you deeper into the city's fascinating museums, gardens and art collections. I've also prepared sections on eating out, shopping and nightlife, with all the practical information you could possibly need for your visit.

Florence itself is slowly beginning to make life for the visitor a little easier. It is a pleasure to walk about the city again, now that traffic has been excluded from parts of the centre. Some problems remain: the opening times of main museums and monuments sometimes seem deliberately designed to frustrate visitors — and perhaps they are, since many Florentines remain deeply ambivalent about the effects of mass tourism on their city. This ambivalence can make them seem haughty and brusque. In reality, Florentines reserve their contempt for those who deserve it and even if, in their hearts, they believe themselves to be a people apart, they can show great warmth and generosity to those who share a love of their city — as I have discovered, and as I hope you will too. **Welcome! Benvenuto! — Christopher Catling**

Contents

Following pages: the Arno,
Ponte Santa Trinita

The year AD1401 marks a watershed in the history of Florence and of Western civilisation. In that year the powerful wool merchants' guild, the *Arte di Calimala*, announced that it would sponsor an artist to make new bronze doors, ornamented with Old Testament scenes, for the city's Baptistry. The aim was to outrival the splendid doors of Pisa's renowned cathedral. This was a highly prestigious project and five leading artists of the day took part in a competition to decide who

15th-century woodcut of Florentine bankers

ultaRe

should design the doors; each was asked to make a bronze relief illustrating the story of Abraham and Isaac.

In the end the judges shortlisted the candidates to two – Lorenzo Ghiberti and Filippo Brunelleschi. Their panels are now displayed in the Bargello Museum (see *Option 1*) and scholars continue to argue, even to this day, over their respective merits. The Florentine merchants decided to honour Ghiberti with the prize, but modern critics prefer Brunelleschi's much more dramatic treatment of the story.

Brunelleschi's panel for the Baptistry doors

Everyone agrees, however, that both artists produced work of revolutionary importance; their bronze reliefs not only demonstrate a new concern for realism, they also convey the full emotive force of this tragic story, in which Abraham is called upon to sacrifice his own son. The two panels mark a decisive shift in the history of artistic expression, rejecting the iconographic formalism of medieval art and looking back to classical Greek and Roman art for inspiration – in other words, the Renaissance, or 'rebirth' was under way.

Milestones of the Renaissance

Of course, Ghiberti and Brunelleschi did not invent this new style of art; rather they reflected the prevailing mood of the age. Florence was, despite constant in-fighting between rival families and with neighbouring cities, a proud, powerful and wealthy city. Florentine prosperity was built on the activities of the city's wool merchants, who traded in raw materials and high-quality cloth

11

Masaccio fresco from the 'Life of St Peter'

throughout Europe. These merchants saw banking as a natural extension of their activities – they invented credit banking and the city's florin became the first common European currency, widely accepted and circulated because of the purity of its gold content.

Dante, who was born in Florence in 1265 and exiled on false charges of corruption in 1302, derided the city as a 'glut of self-made men and quick-got gain'. The Florentines' nascent capitalism may have been distasteful to Dante, but it also fuelled the city's total transformation during the 15th and 16th centuries. Dante's city, whose skyline bristled with defensive towers, like New York in stone, was torn down in favour of new, classically-inspired *palazzi* (palaces). Civic pride was expressed in new churches, libraries, monasteries, hospitals and orphanages, some paid for by guilds or private patrons, others by public taxation.

All this guaranteed a stream of commissions for the artists of the day, many of whom were highly versatile, combining the skills of architect, engineer, painter, sculptor and bronze-caster. Above all, they shared a desire to create art that was appropriate to the self-confident spirit of the age, and in rejecting the stylised religious art of the preceding era they looked to nature and to the world of antiquity for their models and their subject matter.

Within this heady climate, innovations came thick and fast. Brunelleschi, despite losing the Baptistry doors competition, proved his superiority to Ghiberti by building the vast, gravity-defying dome that crowns the cathedral. He solved the problem of how to construct what was then the world's biggest dome by studying the ancient Roman Pantheon, and his structure, soaring above a sea of terracotta roof tiles, has come to symbolise the city.

New depths of realism were achieved by Donatello, whose statue of *St George* made for the guild of armourers in 1416 (now in the Bargello Museum – see *Option 1*) is a superb portrait of human courage tempered by anxiety. Even more startling is his bronze figure of *David*, completed in 1440 (also in the Bargello) the first realistic nude in art since antiquity and one that paved the way for Michelangelo's renowned version of the same subject.

Masaccio blazed a new trail in the technique of perspective in 1425 with his frescos on the *Life of St Peter*, in Santa Maria del Carmine (see *Day 3*) and his precise geometry was rapidly adopted by other artists. Technical innovations underlay many artistic achievements; Luca della Robbia perfected the art of glazed terracotta (see his roundels in the Innocenti orphanage – *Option 2*) and kept the technique a secret, known only to his family, who thereby enriched themselves mightily. Countless other artists developed new paint pigments, which accounts for the astonishing range and brilliance of the colours in the frescos and paintings of artists as diverse as Botticelli (the Uffizi – *Day 1*), Gozzoli (the Medici-Riccardi Palace – *Day 2*), and Pontormo (Santa Felicità church – *Day 3*). Above all, the towering genius of Michelangelo is evident in his huge sculptures, heroic and elemental in scale and subject matter, which have rarely been matched by any artist since.

The Medici

In 1530, Michelangelo was to be found manning the barricades around the church of San Miniato, high above the city of Florence, in a doomed attempt to keep the combined forces of the Medici, the Pope and the Holy Roman Emperor out of the city. Having supervised the hasty construction of temporary fortifications and an artillery platform round the tower of the church, Michelangelo then fled – behaviour that was later forgiven and attributed to his 'artistic temperament'.

Cosimo de' Medici

After stout resistance, the city fell to the Medici and, in 1537, Cosimo I came to power beginning a despotic reign which was to last for 37 years. It was not to be long before the great artists of the age would desert the city, in what Mary McCarthy, author of *The Stones of Florence*, has called 'the great diaspora of artistic talent'. From this point onwards, Florence would cease to be the undisputed centre of artistic excellence, and for the great achievements of the High Renaissance we have to look elsewhere – to Rome and Venice, for example. As if to confirm that Florence had ceased to be pre-eminent in the arts, Giorgio Vasari, court painter and architect to Cosimo I, Grand Duke of Tuscany, published his *Lives of the Artists* in 1550, in effect a final summing-up of the achievements of the past.

It is ironic, then, that this second Cosimo de'Medici presided over a decline in the arts, whereas his predecessors, to whom he was distantly related via the female line, had played such an important role in their encouragement.

The Medici coat of arms is to be seen all over Florence and Tuscany; it consists of six red discs on a field of gold beneath a ducal coronet. Some say the discs represent medicinal pills and that the name, Medici, suggests descent from apothecaries. Others say the discs represent money and are a symbol of the bank founded by

Medici coat of arms

Giovanni di Bicci de'Medici at the beginning of the 15th century. The bank expanded rapidly and was entrusted with the collection of papal revenues, thus laying the foundation of the family fortune.

The first of the family to become actively involved in political life was Giovanni's son, Cosimo de'Medici. Though he preferred not to expose himself to the full glare of public scrutiny, and never sought public office, he proved a very able behind-the-scenes manipulator. Cosimo, and subsequently his grandson, Lorenzo, used their diplomatic skills to bring an end to the costly and inconclusive wars with rival cities that had brought Florence to the verge of bankruptcy. Both thereby helped to create the relatively prosperous and peaceful environment that enabled the city to give birth, simultaneously, to the Renaissance and to humanism.

The humanists were an informal group of like-minded men who shared a common interest in classical philosophy and ideas – one of their number, Aeneas Sylvius Piccolomini, later became Pope Pius II, even though it could be argued that the humanistic emphasis on reason, knowledge and the centrality of man in the scheme of things was incompatible with much Christian dogma.

Cosimo was both a leading member of the humanist circle and its patron – paying for scholars to come to Florence to teach ancient

Latin and Greek, funding the travels of Poggio Bracciolini who specialised in tracking down lost manuscripts, including the works of Cicero, Lucretius and Quintilian. By this means he amassed a huge collection of precious works that were copied, translated and keenly discussed. Some were housed in the public library attached to the monastery of San Marco, others in the Laurentian Library (for both see *Day 2*). Classical ideas rapidly fed through to the artistic community who, already inspired by antique art and architecture, now found that their clients were demanding pictures of mythological, historical and secular subjects – no longer was art exclusively concerned with religious themes, and it greatly benefited from this liberalisation.

Lorenzo de'Medici, soaked in the humanist ideals of his grandfather, proved a worthy successor. He was renowned as a poet and he promoted the study of Dante, Boccaccio and Petrarch in the schools of Florence, thus ensuring that the Tuscan or Florentine dialect, in which these poets wrote, would become the standard for written and spoken Italian from then until the present day.

As a statesman, Lorenzo did much to heal ancient enmities among the rival city states of northern Italy, encouraging the most powerful to form a defensive alliance against the territorial ambitions of Charles VIII of France. Thus, when the much respected Lorenzo died in 1492, Pope Innocent VIII declared, with foresight, 'The peace of Italy is at an end.'

Florence, moreover, was left leaderless; Lorenzo's son, Piero de'Medici, succeeded but when, two years later in 1494, Charles VIII invaded Italy and marched on Florence, Piero simply surrendered the city and then fled. Savonarola, a firebrand preacher, stepped into the vacuum, and succeeded in convincing his fellow Florentines that the city was being punished by God for its preoccupation with profane art and pagan philosophies. He framed a

Savonarola, the firebrand preacher who regarded art as profane

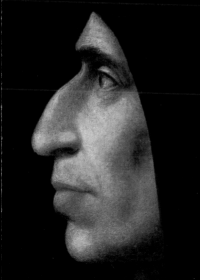

19th-century Florence

republican constitution, founded on strict religious principles, and presided over a brief reign of terror during which petty misdemeanours were punished by torture; the streets blazed with 'bonfires of vanities' on which mirrors, books, paintings, musical instruments and fine clothing – all regarded as ungodly – were burned.

Soon Florence was to witness the sight of Savonarola's own body being consumed by fire. Condemned by the Pope as a heretic and excommunicated, he was arrested, tortured until he pleaded guilty to heresy, and hanged in 1498 – a fire was then lit round the scaffold in Piazza della Signoria.

The republic continued briefly under the leadership of Piero Soderini and his chancellor, Niccolo Machiavelli, but the Medici were determined to regain control of the city – not a difficult task given that Lorenzo de'Medici's second son was crowned as Pope Leo X in 1513. Leo X entered the city in triumph in 1515 and Machiavelli, after a period of imprisonment, retired to write *The Prince*, his reflections on the dirty world of *realpolitik*. Florence made one final attempt to regain its independence – when, in 1530, Michelangelo was put in charge of the city's defences – but, like David pitted against Goliath, the fight was unequal – except that this time, Goliath won.

The City Settles

The city caved in and Alessandro de'Medici was crowned Duke of Florence. He was murdered by his own cousin, Lorenzaccio, and was succeeded by Cosimo I, a ruthless ruler who first set about destroying all his opponents in Florence, then systematically conquering rival cities, such as Siena, to carve out the Grand Duchy of Tuscany. His 'achievements' were recorded by Vasari, whose vainglorious frescos can be seen in the Palazzo Vecchio (*Day 1*). Vasari also built for him the Uffizi (also *Day 1*). To his credit, Cosimo I forced Tuscany into political unity and brought stability to the region – which then played a relatively minor role in world history. Finally, in the 19th century, as people began to appreciate the achievements of the 'pre-Raphaelite' artists, Florence started to become the tourist destination that it is today, renowned throughout the world for its awesome heritage of 15th- and 16th-century art.

Historical Outline

59BC Foundation of the Roman colony of *Florentia*, out of which Florence is to grow.

AD250 The martyrdom of St Minias, to whom a shrine is built on the site of San Miniato church. This is the first (extant) evidence of Christianity in Florence.

4th century Building of Santa Reparata, the city's first cathedral, whose ruins survive in the Duomo (cathedral) crypt.

1125 Florence conquers and destroys the neighbouring city of Fiesole.

13th century Florence is embroiled in factional conflict, siding with the Guelf (pro-Pope) party against Ghibelline (pro-emperor) cities, such as Pisa and Siena, in the struggle for power.

1260 Siena defeats Florence at the battle of Montaperti but is dissuaded from destroying the city itself.

1302 Dante, a victim of the Guelf/Ghibelline conflict, is exiled from Florence and begins his *Divine Comedy*.

1322 The Palazzo Vecchio is completed.

1348 Black Death rages through Europe and kills three-fifths of the population of Florence over the next 50 years. Boccaccio, seeing the effects of the plague in Florence, begins writing his *Decameron*.

1384 Arezzo is captured by the Florentines.

1401 Baptistry doors competition–the start of the *rinascita* (rebirth) or Renaissance.

1406 Florence conquers Pisa and gains a sea port.

1434 Cosimo de'Medici becomes a 'godfather' figure, presiding over the rise of Florence to intellectual and artistic pre-eminence.

1469 Lorenzo de'Medici comes to power.

1494 Savonarola declares Florence a republic ruled only by God.

1498 Execution of Savonarola.

1515 Florence ruled by the Medici Pope, Leo X, then by his cousin, Clement VII.

1527 Rome attacked by imperial troops and Florence rebels against papal rule.

1530 Clement VII and Emperor Charles V sign a peace treaty and unite to hold Florence at siege.

1531 Florence falls.

1555 Cosimo I becomes Duke of Florence and conquers Siena.

1570 Cosimo I made Grand Duke of Tuscany after subjugating the region.

1610 Galileo made court mathematician to Cosimo II.

1631 Galileo excommunicated.

1737 Last Medici Grand Duke dies without an heir. The title passes to the Austrian House of Lorraine.

1808 Annexation of Tuscany by the French empire.

1848 First Italian War of Independence.

1865 Florence becomes temporary capital of the newly united Italy, pending the defeat of Rome.

1916 Mussolini is made prime minister by Victor Emmanuel.

1944 Nazis destroy parts of central Florence. Of the old bridges, only the Ponte Vecchio survives the war.

1946 Italy becomes a republic.

1966 Florence is flooded by the River Arno, triggering a huge restoration programme. Many priceless works of art lost.

1988 Florentines vote for measures to exclude traffic and control air pollution.

Orientation

The *centro storico*, the historic centre, of Florence is very compact and can be crossed on foot in less than half an hour. Hence you will not need to master the complexities of the public transport system and can, instead, delight in the myriad details of the city's ancient *palazzi* as you walk. You are not likely to get lost, since certain landmarks – the dome of the cathedral and the tower of the

By carriage ride through the Piazza della Signoria

Palazzo Vecchio – can be seen from afar, and most of the streets are oriented north-south or east-west.

Street numbering can be confusing until you realise that there are two systems: commercial premises have red numbers and residential premises blue. In written addresses, the letter 'r' after a number stands for *rosso* (red); in other words, a commercial enterprise. In the centre of Florence there are far more commercial premises than residential, so bear in mind that Via Roma 7 (blue), for example, will be considerably further down the street than Via Roma 7r (red).

Opening Times

Unless you master the opening times of Florentine museums and monuments, you could be

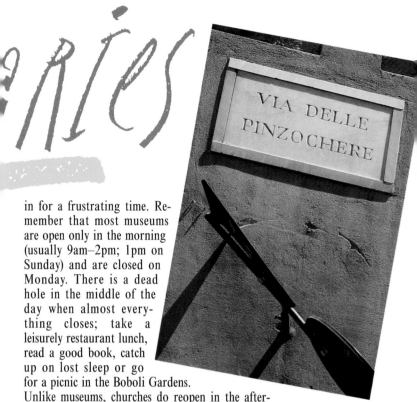

in for a frustrating time. Remember that most museums are open only in the morning (usually 9am–2pm; 1pm on Sunday) and are closed on Monday. There is a dead hole in the middle of the day when almost everything closes; take a leisurely restaurant lunch, read a good book, catch up on lost sleep or go for a picnic in the Boboli Gardens.

Unlike museums, churches do reopen in the afternoon (usually 3.30 or 4pm until 6 or 7pm).

On Sunday afternoon and Monday your choice is even more restricted, since most museums, and many good restaurants, are closed. Do not despair; this guide has been constructed to take opening times into account (alternatively, see the very useful table on page 89 for sights that are open when everything else is closed).

The Duomo and the tower of the Palazzo Vecchio

The Major Landmarks

This first day in Florence will be spent visiting the most famous monuments in the centro storico – the historic centre – including the Duomo (cathedral), the Baptistry, the Piazza della Signoria and Palazzo Vecchio, the Uffizi gallery and the Ponte Vecchio.

The Duomo

If your first day in Florence happens to be a Sunday or Monday you will be able to do only the first part of this tour, since the Palazzo Vecchio and the Uffizi gallery close at 1pm on Sunday and the Uffizi is closed on Monday. Alternative sights will be proposed at appropriate points in the itinerary.

Start in **Piazza del Duomo** (Cathedral Square). The best place for kick-starting yourself into the day with a strong black *espresso* coffee is the **Sergio** bar, Piazzo del Capitolo 1, on the south side of the square, which has seats outside offering good views of the majestic cathedral dome and Giotto's campanile. From here you can get a sense of the huge scale of the cathedral, once the largest church in Christendom, and still the fourth biggest in the world.

The Duomo (from the Latin *Domus Dei*, House of God), was ostensibly built as a place of worship but, just as importantly, it symbolises Florentine civic pride and her citizens' determination always to have the biggest and the best of everything. Hence it is no surprise to learn that it took almost 150 years to build (from 1294 to 1436) and even then the flamboyant neo-Gothic facade, so out of keeping with the classic restraint of the surrounding structures, was not added until the 19th century.

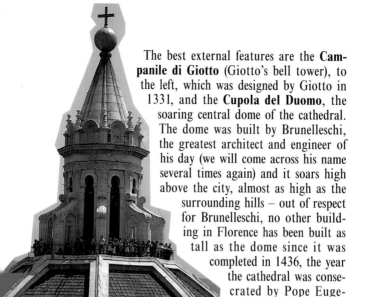

The best external features are the **Campanile di Giotto** (Giotto's bell tower), to the left, which was designed by Giotto in 1331, and the **Cupola del Duomo**, the soaring central dome of the cathedral. The dome was built by Brunelleschi, the greatest architect and engineer of his day (we will come across his name several times again) and it soars high above the city, almost as high as the surrounding hills – out of respect for Brunelleschi, no other building in Florence has been built as tall as the dome since it was completed in 1436, the year the cathedral was consecrated by Pope Eugenius IV.

Pinnacle of the great Brunelleschi dome

If you cross the square from Sergio's, you can enter the cathedral by the door almost opposite, close to Giotto's tower (cathedral open daily 10am–5.30pm, admission free). Once inside, the steps to the left lead down to the **crypt** (open daily except Sunday, 10am–5pm, 3,000 lire). Here you will find Brunelleschi's simple grave. The inscription on the tomb slab compares him to Icarus, the mythical hero who learned to fly but who plunged to his death when he flew too close to the sun, melting his wings. Brunelleschi's is the only tomb in the cathedral – burial within its walls was a singular honour granted in recognition of his genius in building the dome. The rest of the crypt contains the ruins of **Santa Reperata**, the city's first cathedral, built some time in the 4th century AD, and which incorporates Roman remains.

To better appreciate Brunelleschi's architectural achievement, you can climb up to the summit of the cathedral dome. Turn left out of the crypt and right along

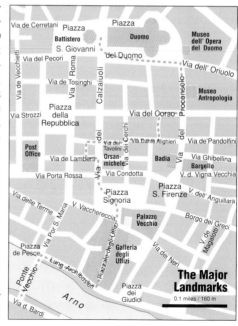

The Major Landmarks

0.1 miles / 160 m

Campanile di Giotto

the north wall of the cathedral. You will pass a famous fresco of **Sir John Hawkwood** on horseback painted by Paulo Uccello in 1436. Hawkwood was an English *condottiere*, or mercenary, whose hired soldiers often fought on behalf of Florence. Other cities honoured their military heroes with equestrian statues in stone or bronze the fact that Hawkwood was commemorated only in a fresco is often cited as an example of Florentine miserliness.

Nearby you will also see a painting of Dante outside the walls of Florence, symbolising his exile – the picture was commissioned in 1465 to commemorate the bicentenary of the poet's birth.

Now you will come to the narrow door that leads up to the **Cupola del Duomo** (open daily except Sunday, 10am–5pm, 5,000 lire). If you climb the 436 steps to the summit you will be rewarded by stunning views and an intimate encounter with the double shell of the dome. Until Brunelleschi, nobody had built such a massive dome since Roman times; he visited Rome to study the 2nd-century AD Pantheon in order to reinvent the ancient technique of building upwards in decreasing circles of interlocking brick.

If you have climbed the dome, you will probably not have the energy to climb the 285 steps of the **Campanile di Giotto**, on the right as you leave the cathedral (open daily 9am–7.30pm in summer, 9am–5pm winter, 5,000 lire). Save this for another day, perhaps, and walk over to the little octagonal **Battistero** (Baptistry) to the west of the cathedral. This has limited opening hours (Monday to Saturday 1–6pm, Sunday 9am–1pm, admission free) but no matter – it is the exterior that is really important. Set into this 10th-century building, one of the oldest in Florence, are three sets

Scooters in the piazza

of bronze doors. Those to the south were made in the 1330s by the Pisan artist Andrea Pisano, and illustrate the *Life of St John the Baptist*, patron saint of Florence. Already they exhibit Renaissance characteristics – dynamism in the dramatic grouping of figures, fluency and immediacy, all in contrast to the rather static spirituality of the Gothic art of the 13th and 14th centuries. Pisano was several decades ahead of his time.

The Renaissance proper is conventionally dated to 1401 when a competition was held to select an artist for the remaining doors (see *History and Culture*). Ghiberti, the winner, first made the doors that fill the north entrance, illustrating New Testament scenes, completed in 1424. He then made the superb **Paradise Door** (Porta del Paradiso) or the east entrance facing the cathedral, so called because Michelangelo hailed these doors as suitable for the entrance to paradise. What you see now are casts of the original panels, illustrating Old Testament scenes (the originals, completed in 1452, are now under restoration and will eventually be displayed in the Museo dell'Opera del Duomo – see *Option 3*). The doorframes, however, are original and contain portrait busts of 24 leading Renaissance artists – Ghiberti himself is the bald-headed figure, third up from the bottom in the centre of the doors.

Renaissance man?

When you have seen enough, walk down the south flank of the cathedral, to the east end, and turn right down Via del Proconsolo. On the left you will pass No 12, the **Palazzo Nonfinito** (the Unfinished Palace) begun by Bountalenti in 1593 and never completed; it contains the **Anthropology Museum** (open Thursday, Friday, Saturday and the third Sunday in every month, 9am–1pm, admission free) with interesting relics of Captain Cook's last voyage to the Pacific. Take the first right, Via del Corso, passing the **Banco di Toscana** (Bank of Tuscany) on the right – the exchange rate here is good and the banking hall features a fresco of the Virgin, St John and St Zenobius.

Opposite the bank, go through a tunnel into Via Santa Margherita where, on the left, is the little church built in 1200 where Dante first set eyes on Beatrice Portinare, the daughter of a wealthy banker, whom he was to idealise in his poetry. The church is often used for baroque chamber music and organ recitals – see the notice at the entrance (church open Monday to Friday 9am–noon and 3–6.30pm, Sunday 9am–noon, admission free).

At the end of the street, on the right, is the **Casa di Dante** (open Monday to Saturday 9.30am–12.30pm and 3.30–6.30pm, Sunday 9.30am–12.30pm, closed Wednesday, 4,000 lire). This much

restored medieval house with its truncated 13th-century tower is claimed as Dante's birthplace and contains a small museum on the poet's life and work–the downstairs rooms (entrance free) are often used for exhibitions of contemporary art.

Turn right in Via Dante Alighieri and head straight on, ignoring side turnings, to Via de' Calzaiuoli (passing the renowned ice-cream shop, Perche Noi, on the left at Via de' Tavolina 19r). Opposite now is the church of **Orsanmichele** (open daily 8am–noon and 3–6.30pm, admission free). Walk round the church, to the right, down Via dei Tavolini, to study the statues in the wall niches. Each niche belonged to one of the city's powerful guilds, who commissioned artists to portray their patron saints – the most famous statue, Donatello's *St George*, is now replaced by a copy and the

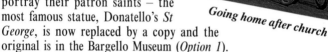

Going home after church

original is in the Bargello Museum (*Option 1*).

At the back, Orsanmichele is linked to the 13th-century Palazzo del'Arte della Lana (Wool Guild Palace) by an aerial corridor. The entrance to the church is below and its centrepiece is Andrea Orcagna's elaborate tabernacle (1459), decorated with scenes from the *Life of the Virgin*, enclosing Bernardo Daddi's painting of the *Madonna* (1347). Turn left out of the church, left again in Via de' Lamberti, passing Donatello's statue of *St Mark* in the first niche, then right in Via de' Calzaiuoli, to **Piazza della Signoria**.

By contrast with the narrow medieval streets, the sheer size of this vast (and now traffic-free) square has great impact. Towering over everything is the battlemented facade and campanile of the **Palazzo Vecchio**, built as the seat of city government between 1299 and 1322. This dwarfs even the huge heroic figure of *David* (a copy – Michelangelo's original is in the Accademia, see *Day 2*), Bandinelli's rather lumpy figure of *Hercules* (1534) and the licentious nymphs of Ammanati's *Neptune Fountain* (1575). These works of art, all fronting the palace, symbolise Florence in various ways – David as a figure of defiance against tyranny, Hercules as the mythical founder of the city and Neptune as a metaphor for the city's naval fleet created by Cosimo I. To the right, sheltering under the **Loggia dei Lanzi** (named after Cosimo I's bodyguard, the lancers) are several antique statues and Giambologna's renowned *Rape of the Sabine Women* (1583).

Some decisions are now necessary. If you fancy lunch try **Orcagne**, Piazza della Signoria 1 (Tel: 292188, closed Monday) or the cheaper **Pizzeria il David** next door (No 2). Both offer good views

The towering Palazzo Vecchio

A fresco in the Palazzo Vecchio

of the square from their pavement terraces. **Rivoire** alongside (No 5r) offers a classy ambience for ice-cream or pastries (Tel: 214412, closed Monday). Alternatively, dive down the alley called Chiasso dei Baroncelli to **Monkey Business** (Tel: 288219, closed Sunday), a jungle-theme restaurant serving expensive but out-standing *nouvelle cuisine* or traditional Tuscan food.

Your choice will partly depend on the day of the week – as will your next move. The afternoon will be spent visiting the Palazzo Vecchio and the Uffizi but not if it is a Sat-urday, when the Palazzo Vecchio is closed: instead you might like to visit the Bargello (*Option 1*) or spend longer in the Uffizi. If it is a Sunday afternoon, when both are closed, you might like to walk off lunch by heading for San Miniato (*Option 5*), as Floren-tines do on a Sunday. If it is Monday, you can visit the Palazzo Vecchio, but not the Uffizi; instead, try the excellent Museo dell'Opera del Duomo (*Option 3*).

After lunch you cross the Piazza della Signoria again, negotiat-ing the crowds, the pigeons and the horse-drawn carriages. Passing *David*, climb the steps of the **Palazzo Vecchio** to enter the delight-ful *cortile* (entrance courtyard) with its charming *putto* and dolphin fountain, Vasari's copy of an original made by Verrocchio in 1470. This courtyard is gracefully feminine and its frescos, by Vasari, de-pict Austrian cities to make Joanna of Austria feel at home on the occasion of her marriage to Francesco de'Medici in 1565.

The cortile of the Palazzo Vecchio

Upstairs, though, the tone is aggressively masculine, as you will find as you turn right up the steps that lead to the **Quartieri Monumentali** (open Monday to Friday 9am–7pm, Sunday 8am–1pm, closed Saturday, 10,000 lire). The first room is the vast Salone dei Cinquecento, used for meetings of the Florentine Grand Council under the reign of Savonarola, but later transformed by Vasari whose frescos depict the military victories of Duke Cosimo I. Statues of writhing, wrestling figures, by Michelangelo, Vincenzo de'Rossi and Giambologna line the walls. Just off is the little **Studiolo** (study) of Francesco de'Medici, dating to 1575, a suitable retreat for the reclusive prince whose parents, Duke Cosimo I and Eleonora di Toledo, are de-

The magnificient Sala dei Gigli

picted on the walls. Beyond lies a whole suite of rooms, all frescoed by Vasari, used by the various Medici Popes and one-time rulers of Florence; several offer fine views over the city. The rooms of Eleonora di Toledo are among the most attractive, with their ceiling frescos depicting feminine virtue.

After this comes the most magnificent of all the chambers, the **Sala dei Gigli**, whose walls are covered in the gold fleur-de-lis (lily) symbol of Florence. Here, too, you will find a delicate marble statue of St John the Baptist (patron saint of Florence) as a boy, and Donatello's *Judith and Holofernes* (1460), originally placed in the Piazza della Signoria after the expulsion of the Medici in 1494 – once again a biblical story (the virtuous Judith slaying the drunken tyrant Holofernes)

was used to symbolise Florentine triumph over despotism. Just off this is the **Cancellaria**, with a painting and a bust of Niccolo Machiavelli who used the room as his office whilst chancellor.

Steps now lead down and out of the Palazzo Vecchio; returning through the *cortile*, exit and turn left for the entrance to the **Galleria degli Uffizi** (open Tuesday to Saturday 9am–7pm, Sunday 9am–1pm, closed Monday, 10,000 lire). This complex was built by Vasari, from 1560, to house the administrative offices of Duke

The Ponte Vecchio, built in 1345 and occupied by jewellers' shops since 1593

Cosimo I (hence its name – *uffici* simply means offices) as well as the artistic masterpieces commissioned or collected by the Medici. The art collection is outstanding and includes antique statuary, displayed in the corridors, while the paintings, displayed chronologically in the side room, include some of the world's most famous early Renaissance works. The damage caused by the 1993 terrorist bomb was less serious than at first thought. The star is Botticelli, whose restored allegory of spring, *Primavera* (1480), and *Birth of Venus* (1485) are displayed in Room X. Exhaustion sets in about halfway round the gallery, but you can refresh yourself in the café (at the end of the west corridor, beyond Room XLV) which sits over the Loggia dei Lanzi with good views of the Piazza della Signoria. Save some time to see the later works in the west wing, especially those of Titian (Room XXVII) and Caravaggio (XLII).

From the Uffizi exit, turn right down to the river Arno and right again to reach the **Ponte Vecchio** (old bridge), the 'golden bridge' of Florence. Wander with the crowds, enjoying the views from the bridge and the bustle of traders, tourists and buskers.

For a guide to the best shops on the bridge see the *Shopping* section of this book. There are also scores of good restaurants nearby – just south of the bridge you can dine elegantly *al fresco* in Piazza Santa Felicità at **Celestino** (Tel: 296574) or **Di Bibo** (Tel: 298554); alternatively you can eat authentic and inexpensive pizza at **Borgo Antic** (see *Eating Out*, or at the **Pizzeria Dante**, Piazza Nazario Sauro (just south of the Ponte alla Carraia, Tel: 293215).

Detail from Botticelli's 'Birth of Venus'

Michelangelo and the Medici

Today you will hit the Michelangelo trail, visiting some of his best works and unravelling his somewhat ambivalent relationship with the Medici family; in between you will visit the markets around San Lorenzo and some very upmarket shops in the Santa Maria Novella district.

Head straight for the **Galleria dell'Accademia**, Via Ricasoli 60 (open Tuesday to Saturday 9am–2pm, Sunday 9am–1pm, closed Monday, 10,000 lire). Aim to get there just before the 9am opening time, if possible, because this gallery attracts a huge number of visitors and long queues rapidly build up, especially at Easter and in the peak summer months. If there is already a queue, don't despair – it moves quite quickly and you should not have to wait much more than 15 minutes to get in (if you've time for a coffee try the typical neighbourhood bar on the corner of Via Ricasoli and Via degli Alfani, just south of the Accademia entrance).

The queues can be explained in two words: Michelangelo's *David* (1504) – the original statue, as opposed to the copy that now stands in front of the Palazzo Vecchio. Its current setting is far from satisfactory – it was moved here in 1873 as a precaution

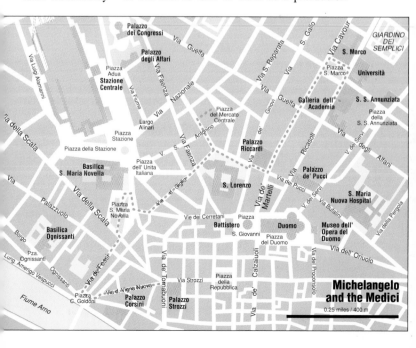

against weathering and pigeon droppings – but the towering figure still exerts a magnetic force. *David* is both a powerful celebration of the adolescent male body (though somewhat distorted, with overlarge head and hands) and a symbol of Florentine aspiration – her citizens liked to think of themselves as brave combatants, ready to fight any tyrannical Goliath who threatened their liberty (for which read the Pope, the Medici, the Holy Roman Emperor, neighbouring city states or any other temporary enemy).

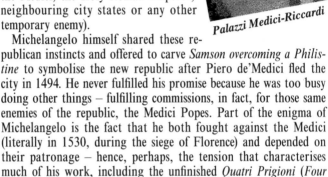

Palazzi Medici-Riccardi

Michelangelo himself shared these republican instincts and offered to carve *Samson overcoming a Philistine* to symbolise the new republic after Piero de'Medici fled the city in 1494. He never fulfilled his promise because he was too busy doing other things – fulfilling commissions, in fact, for those same enemies of the republic, the Medici Popes. Part of the enigma of Michelangelo is the fact that he both fought against the Medici (literally in 1530, during the siege of Florence) and depended on their patronage – hence, perhaps, the tension that characterises much of his work, including the unfinished *Quatri Prigioni* (*Four Slaves*) displayed here. These were originally intended for the tomb of Pope Julius II. In their unfinished state they still express powerfully the sense of enslavement, as the half-formed figures struggle to release themselves from their imprisonment in stone.

Michelangelo's work is the highlight of the Accademia, but there are some other interesting works – in particular, do not miss the excellent plaster models made by Lorenzo Burtolini (1797–1850) displayed in the **Salone delle Toscane**. These are preliminary working models, which were then copied in sculpted marble to produce the final work of art, and they include outstanding portrait busts and funerary monuments.

From the Accademia, turn right and head for the **Piazza San Marco**. If it is term time you will weave your way through chatting groups of art students who are study-

A student at the Accademia

ing at the Accademia, which was founded by Vasari, with Michelangelo as one of its members, in 1563. You will also pass, almost opposite the gallery exit, the Libreria LEF bookshop (Via Ricasoli 105); if you are interested in art and architecture you will find a comprehensive stock of books, postcards and posters here.

Straight ahead, in the square, is the **Museo di San Marco** (open Tuesday to Saturday 9am–2pm, Sunday 9am–1pm, closed Monday, 6,000 lire) housed in a group

Detail of Michelangelo's 'David'

of conventual buildings. Many famous names are connected with San Marco. Cosimo de'Medici paid for the building of this monastery, which was occupied by Dominican friars from the nearby hill town of Fiesole in 1436. Fra Angelico spent most of his life within its walls and the museum contains most of his paintings, as well as some superb frescos: his *Crucifixion* (1442) in the Chapter House, his *Annunciation* at the top of the staircase leading to the dormitory, and a series of almost abstract pictures, designed as aids to religious contemplation, in cells 1 to 10 of the dormitory (other artists were involved in the remaining cell paintings). Savonarola was made prior of the convent in 1491 and his cells (Nos 12 to 14) contain various mementoes.

As you emerge from San Marco, look to the right-hand (northwestern) corner of the square, where there is a house ornamented with rams' heads. This stands on the site of the Medici garden in which Cosimo de'Medici displayed his collection of antique sculptures and where, in the attached school of art, the young Michelangelo studied drawing.

Now head down Via Cavour to reach No 1, the **Palazzi Medici-Riccardi**, on the right. This somewhat grim (and deliberately unostentatious) palace was built for Cosimo de'Medici between 1444 and 1464. It was from here than Cosimo and his heirs operated as unofficial rulers of Florence until Piero fled the city in 1494. The building is undergoing restoration, but you can go into the courtyards, whose walls are studded with antique inscriptions. If, by the time you visit, the **Cappella dei Magi** is open again, do go in and see the stunningly colourful fresco of the *Journey of the Magi*; this was painted by Benozzo Gozzoli in 1459 and members of the

Cappella dei Principi

Medici family are depicted amongst the royal retinue.

Leaving the palace, turn right and right again, in Via de'Gori, and you will plunge into the midst of the huge and bustling San Lorenzo street market. There will be time to explore this later – for now the aim is to see the church of San Lorenzo and the Medici tombs before they close. As you weave through the stalls you will see an equestrian statue of *Giovanni delle Bande Nera*, the warrior father of Duke Cosimo I, by Bandinelli (1540).

To the left of the statue, **San Lorenzo** is entered through a door in the rough unfinished facade (open daily 7am–noon and 3.30–5.30pm, admission free). The interior is a supreme example of early Renaissance classicism, principally designed by Brunelleschi from 1423 and remarkable for the elegant sobriety of the grey stone and white walls. Just before the central domed crossing are two huge marble pulpits carved by Donatello with scenes from the *Passion* and *Resurrection of Christ*. To the north of the pulpits, Bronzino's huge fresco, depicting the *Martyrdom of St Lawrence* (1569), is unmissable. To the left, and often overlooked, is a more recent painting by Pietro Annigoni (1910–88) of the young Jesus with Joseph in a carpenter's workshop.

Between the two a doorway leads out to the serene cloister, with views over to Giotto's campanile, and immediately to the right a staircase leads up to the **Biblioteca Laurenziana**, or Laurentian Library (open Monday to Saturday 10am–noon, closed Sunday, admission free). The library, with its extraordinary vestibule and staircase, was designed by Michelangelo from 1524. His client was the Medici Pope, Clement VII, and the library was built to house part of the famous collection of antique Greek and Latin manuscripts collected by Cosimo and Lorenzo de'Medici. The smell of old wood still pervades the library and occasional exhibitions are mounted to show off the treasures of this outstanding collection.

Return through the church, turn left at the exit doors and weave round to the rear of San Lorenzo for the last, and perhaps greatest, example of Michelangelo's work for the Medici. The entrance to the **Cappelle Medicee** (Medici Chapels) is on Piazza Madonna degli Aldobrandini (open Tuesday to Saturday 9am–2pm, Sunday 9am–1pm, closed Monday, 9,000 lire).

When you enter you will first pass through the extraordinary **Cappella dei Principi** (Chapel of the Princes), whose walls are cov-

ered in costly multi-coloured marble and whose enormous sarcophagi commemorate the 16th- and 17th-
century Grand Dukes of Tuscany. From here a corridor leads to the **Sagrestia Nuova** (New Sacristy) designed by Michelangelo – sober by contrast and yet
containing some stupendous sculptures.

The modest tomb of Lorenzo de'Medici is marked
by Michelangelo's unfinished *Madonna and Child*.
To the left is the tomb of Lorenzo's grandson,
also called Lorenzo (1492-1519), draped with the
figures of *Dawn* and *Dusk*, while opposite is the
tomb of Lorenzo's son, Giuliano, with the figures
of *Night* and *Day*. These awesome figures, symbolising the temporal and the eternal forces of
nature, were carved fitfully between 1520 and
1533. Ironically, whilst still working on them,
Michelangelo was, at the same time, involved
in the battle to keep Florence an independent

In the Mercato Centrale

republic against the besieging forces of the Medici.
When that battle was lost it is thought that Michelangelo hid from
his Medici patrons in this very chapel. A small room (usually kept
locked, but you can try asking an attendant) contains charcoal
sketches on the walls made by Michelangelo at this time.

From the sombre mood of the Medici Chapel, you plunge back
into the mêlée of Florentine street life. If you want to eat, turn left

into Via del Giglio,
where there is a good
choice of restaurants.
Ganesh, at 28r, is a
smart Indian restaurant
serving mild curries, tan-
doori and vegetarian
dishes (Tel: 289694,
closed Monday and Tues-
day). Opposite, at 49r, is
the upmarket **Gran Ris-
torante de'Medici** where
you can eat a full-blown
bistecca alla fiorentina,
or a simple pizza (Tel:
218778, closed Monday).
If you are on a budget,
then try the Chinese
restaurants on the west
side of Piazza Santa
Maria Novella for bar-
gain prices and a table
in the open air.

Alternatively, you can

Straw hats for sale

snack in the Central Market – in which case turn right out of the Medici Chapel, then left in Via dell'Ariento, passing through the San Lorenzo market. The stalls immediately adjacent to the church are geared to tourists and sell T-shirts, leatherwork and souvenirs. The further in you get, the more the stalls cater to the needs of ordinary Florentines, selling bargain-priced clothes, shoes, fabrics and table linen.

Not long ago (1990) the city administration tried to close the market down – at least, that part of the market that crowds around San Lorenzo church. The police gave up in the face of determined resistance from the stallholders. As you walk through, do not neglect the little shops either side of the street, almost hidden by the stalls, where you will find all sorts of necessities for sale.

Halfway up, on the right, is the entrance to the huge **Mercato Centrale** (Central Market). The stalls on the ground floor sell an abundance of meat, fish and cheese, while upstairs, under the glass and cast-iron roof, you can buy fruit, vegetables and flowers – and you will not find better quality or keener prices than here. You can also sample some Florentine specialities sold from the cooked-meat stalls or cafés downstairs – *lampredotto* (pig's intestine) or *trippa* (tripe) eaten with *panino* (bread roll) are perhaps not to everyone's taste, but *porchetta* (roast suckling pig) is delicious.

Having explored the market, or strolled along the Arno embankment to fill the siesta hours, head for **Piazza Santa Maria Novella** and its **church** (open daily 7–11.30am and 3.30–6pm, admission free). There is plenty to see here to fill an hour or so. The vast square itself was once used for chariot races and the church has a graceful facade of green and white marble, incorporating the name of the Rucellai family along with their symbol or trademark – a billowing ship's sail, representing trade. The wealthy family, who paid the architect Alberti to build the facade in 1470, formed a marriage alliance with the Medici – hence you will also see that family's ring-and-ostrich-feather symbol amongst the complex geometric patterning.

Inside, on the wall of the third chapel on the left, is Masaccio's renowned fresco of the *Trinity, Mary and St John* (1427), whose architectural setting and three-dimensional qualities make it a landmark in the development of perspective

Not a good place to sit

in early Renaissance art. Behind the high altar are the charming and colourful frescos of Ghirlandaio, illustrating the *Life of the Virgin* and of *St John the Baptist* (1485-90). These repay detailed study and give a good idea of the clothing worn by well-to-do Florentines in the late 15th century, and the richness of their houses. Equally compelling are Filippino Lippi's frescos in the Strozzi Chapel, to the right of the altar (1497–1502).

There are more frescos of note in the cloister alongside the church, including Uccello's dramatic *Noah and the Flood* (1450) but you will have to return another time to see this, thanks to perverse opening times (cloister open Monday to Saturday 9am–2pm, Sunday 8am–1pm, closed Friday, 4,000 lire). For now, head left across the square, into Piazza degli Ottavioni and Via de' Fossi. The latter boasts some interesting shops. **Saleh** (65r) sells good modern jewellery, **Neri** (57r) sells antiques and **G. Lisio** (41r) makes and sells superb handwoven textiles and tapestries. At **Antonio Frilli** (26r) you can buy reproduction sculptures of the most famous statues in Florence, in every imaginable size, plus fountains in marble, erotic groups in the style of Canova and some original art nouveau works – most, though, are priced in millions of lire.

At the bottom of the street, leading to Piazza C Goldoni, there are more good shops worth investigating: in Borgo Ognissanti, to the right, they include the **BM** English-language bookshop (4r) and **Fallani Best** (15r) which sells art nouveau and art deco pieces. Alternatively, turning left brings you to Via della Vigna Nuova and Via de' Tornabuoni, both lined with chic boutiques and couturiers (see *Shopping*). If you can resist spending too much money, then reward yourself with a table for tonight in the elegant setting of the **Cantinetta Antinori**, at the top of Via de' Tornabuoni (see *Eating Out*) or seek out the rather Gothic setting of **Trattoria Garga** (Via del Moro 48r, Tel: 298898, closed Monday). The décor here is definitely freakish but the atmosphere is lively and the cooking highly creative.

Oltrarno: Pitti Palace and Boboli Gardens

Today's itinerary heads south to Oltrarno – literally 'beyond the Arno' – to visit the Pitti Palace, with its five museums, the Boboli Gardens for outstanding views, and the Brancacci Chapel for Masaccio's great frescos on the Life of St Peter.

Cross the river by the **Ponte Vecchio** (literally 'Old Bridge'), built in its present form in 1345 and the only one in the city that did not get blown up in August 1944 by retreating Nazis (the others have since been reconstructed).

As you cross the bridge, note the aerial corridor on the left-hand side, high above the jewellers' shops. This is known as the **Corridoio Vasariano** (Vasari's Corridor), named after its designer, and it links the Palazzo Vecchio, seat of the Tuscan administration, with the Palazzo Pitti, home of the Medici Grand Dukes from 1550. The rulers of Florence and Tuscany could walk along this corridor without having to sully themselves by contact with their subjects. On the opposite side of the river, as you walk down Via de' Guicciardini, you will see the corridor again as it runs in front of **Santa Felicità** church, on the left.

Have a look inside this church, which has two remarkable works

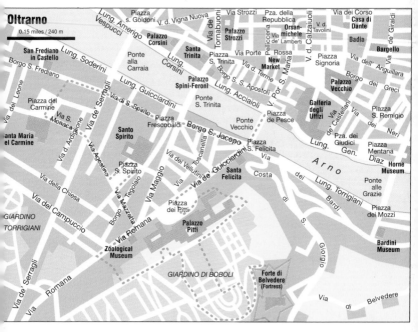

by the Mannerist artist, Pontormo, an *Annunciation* and a *Deposition* (both of 1525–28). Mary Mc-Carthy (in *The Stones of Florence*) professed to find these works decadent, but she accurately described their extraordinary colours – peppermint pink, orchid, gold-apricot, pomegranate and iridescent salmon!

Continue on past the Palazzo Guicciardini (No 15) with its glimpse of a lovely courtyard garden, and settle for a coffee in the very smart **Bar Pitti** (Piazza dei Pitti 35r) while you take in the vast edifice opposite.

The Pitti Palace

The **Palazzo Pitti** (Pitti Palace) was begun in the late 1450s for the banker Luca Pitti, but the cost of the building brought him to the verge of bankruptcy and his heirs sold it to Eleonora di Toledo, the Spanish-born wife of Duke Cosimo I, in 1549. The Medici moved here in 1550 and from then onwards it served as the home of Tuscany's rulers, gradually being expanded to its present immense bulk. It now houses three museums, and there are two more in the Boboli Gardens behind. You would have to be a glutton for punishment to see them all. We will spend the morning in the **Galleria Palatina** (Palatine Gallery), which contains outstanding works of art (open Tuesday to Saturday 9am–2pm, Sunday 9am–1pm, closed Monday, 8,000 lire). If, however, you are interested in court and theatrical costume, you should visit the excellent **Galleria del Costume** (same hours, 6,000 lire). This is located in the east wing of the palace, but can be entered only from the Boboli Gardens – you must, however obtain your ticket in advance, from the main ticket office (*Biglietteria*); you will find this by entering the central archway at the front of the palace and turning left in the inner courtyard.

The entrance to the first-floor Galleria Pala-

Bust on the Ponte Vecchio

38

tina lies to the right of the courtyard where a flight of steps leads up to a suite of apartments with frescos by Pietro da Cortona (1641-65). They illustrate, allegorically, the stages in the education of a prince as he leaves behind the joys of adolescent love (symbolised by a pneumatic Venus) to learn the arts of science, war, and justice under the respective tutelage of Apollo, Mars and Jupiter. Apart from these rich frescos, each room contains a wealth of art. In the Sala de Venere (Venus), for example, look out for Titian's portrait of a woman known as *La Bella* (the Beautiful), painted in 1536, and Canova's statue of *Venus* emerging from her bath.

The opulence of the palace

In the Sala di Apollo is another Titian, the rather more erotic than repentant *Maddalena* (Mary Magdalene). Rubens's vast canvas, the *Consequences of War* (1638), is the highlight of the Sala di Marte (Mars), a bleak allegory of the atrocities being perpetrated in Europe at the time of the Thirty Years' War. Far more serene is Raphael's *Donna Valeta* (1516), said to be a portrait of Lucrezia delle Rovere, in the Sala di Giove (Jove), and the same artist's tender *Madonna della Seggiola* (1515) in the Sala di Saturna (Saturn).

The numerous rooms that lie beyond are remarkable for the opulence of their decorations. In particular, do not miss Napoleon's bathroom, designed in 1813 as a part of a suite of apartments for the Emperor after he had conquered northern Italy. It is decorated with stucco nymphs and four marble Nereids – who would not love such a sumptuous bathroom as this?

Even so, the weight of crimson, gold and heavy ornate furniture can become oppressive after a while, and it is a relief to escape back into the palace courtyard and head for the open green spaces of the **Giardino di Boboli**, or Boboli Gardens (open Tuesday to Sunday, 9am–4.30pm in November to February, 9am–5.30pm March and October, 9am–6.30pm April, May and September, 9am–7.30pm

June to August, closed Monday, entrance free). These are among the largest and most splendid formal gardens in Italy and they were laid out from 1550 onwards. To enter the gardens, exit from the palace courtyard, turn right to follow the palace facade and go through the small arch straight ahead.

Time-keeper on Forte Belved[ere]

Just inside the entrance, on the left, is a humorous marble statue of Duke Cosimo's court dwarf riding on a turtle. Straight ahead is a somewhat fantastical grotto whose inner walls are decorated with sheep, goats and shepherds playing among the stalactites. Rather incongruously, Michelangelo's unfinished carvings of the *Four Slaves* were placed here too by Duke Cosimo (today they have been replaced by copies – the originals are in the Accademia – see *Day 2*). Further inside you will come across *Paris seducing Helen of Troy* in Vincenzo de'Rossi's erotic marble grouping and, almost hidden from view, Giambologna's delicious *Venus* emerging from her bath.

Take the steps to the right of the grotto and follow the broad path uphill, keeping right where the path divides, to reach the grand theatrical space at the rear of the Pitti Palace, surrounded by the green of holm oaks and cypress. Head up the central avenue, left, past an ancient Egyptian obelisk. It is quite a climb to the next terrace, where there is a pool and a statue of Neptune spearing fish, as well as a good backward view. Turn left, then right to reach the statue of *Abundance* beneath the walls of the **Forte Belvedere** built by Duke Ferdinando in 1590. If you turn left and follow the path beneath the fortress walls you will eventually come

The carefully constructed Boboli Gardens

to a gate and a path leading down, to the left, to the little baroque **Kaffeehaus** (open 10am–5.30pm) built in 1776. The interior is frescoed with garden scenes and the intimate terrace alongside makes a perfect spot for lunch. The Kaffeehaus serves pizza, sandwiches, ice-cream and drinks and the views from the terrace cover the whole of the city (there are also toilets here).

Alternatively, you can lunch in the centre of Forte Belvedere where there is a small bar serving sandwiches and pizza. To reach the fort, return up the path to the gate, pass through it and take the steps to the right (open daily 9am–8pm in summer, 9am–5pm in winter, admission free).

The fort is well named, for the views from its walls really are beautiful; in one direction you look over the whole of the city centre whilst in the other you look over a rural landscape of olive groves and cypress trees to the church of San Miniato and up to the ancient astronomical observatory, the Torre del Gallo.

After lunch, retrace your steps all the way back to the statue of *Abundance*

Mischievous stonework in the Boboli Gardens

and continue straight on, past the gardeners' houses, until you reach the top of the **Viottolone dei Cipressi** (Cypress Avenue) which focuses your view down towards the Via Roma, with the hills of Bellosguardo rising to the right. Turn your back on the avenue and take the path to the left, past a broken column, then descend by the path to the right which takes you down to the rear of the Pitti Palace again (the doorway flanked by two lions leads to the **Galleria del Costume**, the Costume Gallery). Turn left to descend a wide avenue and take the first right to exit the garden into Via Romana. Turn right and walk up this street, taking the third turning left, Via Mazzetta; you may want to browse for a while in the many good antique shops in this area, especially in Via Maggio. Via Mazzetta leads to the leafy **Piazza Santo Spirito** where, depending on the time of day, you might find a street market in full swing.

This part of the city is very different from the historic centre north of the river – bustling, lively and authentically Florentine. Walking along the right-hand side of the square, note **Caffe Ricchi** (9r) with its tables and chairs under the trees; you may want to return here for an evening drink and dinner in the **Trattoria Borgo Antic** (6r). Next door you can watch carpenters at work producing intricate mouldings for reproduction furniture while the antique shop **Il Tempo** (1r) sells toys and 1950s memorabilia. At the head of the square is the church of **Santo Spirito** (open daily 8am–noon and 4pm–6pm, admission free). This is regarded as Brunelleschi's masterpiece, a superb example of Renaissance classicism with a serene interior, begun in 1436.

Leaving the church, walk up the right-hand side of the square. If you have fallen in love with Florence, take a look at the real-estate agent, **R Agostini** (19r) to see if any apartment takes your fancy – small flats for a mere 200 million lire. The workshop at 17r makes lovely reproduction baroque picture frames and the **Antica Trattoria Oreste** (16r) is another potential dinner spot.

Turn right in Via Sant'Agustino, past tempting food shops and the little bookshop at 42r which has a display of Edwardian erotic postcards in the window – plump matrons playing at being the Three Graces. Cross Via de' Serraglio (the name does not refer to seraglios, or brothels, but to the Serragli family) and continue down Via Santa Monica to reach the huge **Piazza del Carmine**. The church of Santa Maria del Carmine was destroyed by fire in

Erotic postcards in Via Sant'Agustino

1771 and rebuilt. However, by great good fortune, the **Cappella Brancacci**, alongside to the right, was spared (open Monday–Saturday 10am–5pm, Sunday 1–5pm, closed Tuesday, 5,000 lire). Once inside this tiny chapel you are brought face to face with the newly restored frescos on the *Life of St Peter* begun by Masolino, continued by Masaccio from 1425 until his death in 1428 and completed by Filippino Lippi in 1480. Masaccio's contribution has been hailed as a superb example of the emerging Renaissance style, remarkable for the clearly worked out perspective and the use of *chiaroscuro*, light and shade, to highlight the central figures. St Peter, a serene figure in a

A social afternoon in the piazza

saffron toga and blue tunic, moves amongst the poor and the crippled, distributing alms and working miracles, against the backdrop of the streets and buildings of 15th-century Florence. So intimate is the space, and so forceful the work, that you will feel part of the crowd that witnesses these events.

Masaccio's work is mainly in the upper tier of the fresco and includes his vigorous and dramatic *Expulsion from Paradise*, in which the figures of Adam and Eve, no longer beautiful as in Masolino's *Temptation* scene opposite, are racked with misery. The scenes in the lower tier, mostly by the artist Filippino Lippi, are equally distinguished but it is Masaccio, inevitably, who wins all the praise for his pioneering work and youthful genius (Masaccio was a mere 27 years old when he died).

Piazza Santo Spirito

Leaving the chapel, cross the square to the right, passing **Dolce Vita** (6r) – a popular night spot (see the section in this book on *Nightlife*). As I have already noted, there are plenty of good spots in this district for enjoying an evening drink or meal – or you can return to the Ponte Vecchio by turning right in Borgo San Frediano and just following your nose.

Option 1. The Bargello and Santa Croce

This morning's visit is to an outstanding collection of sculpture in the Bargello Museum; you can also sample the world's best ice-cream and pay homage at the tombs of Galileo, Machiavelli and Michelangelo.

Start in the **Piazza di San Firenze**. If you take coffee in the tiny **Bar Nazionale** (No 7r) your breakfast companions are likely to be lawyers who work in the law courts of the **Tribunale**, the baroque building on the opposite side of the bustling square. This corner of Florence has always been associated with enforcement of the law; the Bargello, which you are about to visit, once served as the city prison and place of execution.

First, though, make a quick detour to the **Badia Fiorentina**, the church opposite the Bargello on the corner of Via de Proconsolo and Via Dante Alighieri. Inside you will find a delightful painting by Filippino Lippi, the *Apparition of the Virgin to St Bernard* (1485). Now try the door immediately to the right of the high altar; if it is open, walk up the stairs to the peaceful **Chiostro degli Aranci** (named after the orange trees that, sadly, no longer grow here). The lovely cloister, with damaged 15th-century frescos, offers fine views of the Badia's six-sided Romanesque campanile.

Bronze bird at the Bargello

Leave the Badia and cross to the **Bargello** (Tuesday–Saturday 9am–2pm, Sunday 9am–1pm, closed Monday, 6,000 lire). The noble inner courtyard, where criminals were once tortured and executed, is now a peaceful spot whose walls are studded with *stelle* (carved armorial stones). The room on the right contains a rich col-

lection of 16th-century sculpture; Michelangelo's first great work, the *Drunken Bacchus* (1499), seems to stagger off his pedestal.

A stately external staircase leads up to the first floor loggia where there is an amusing display of bronze birds made by Giambologna for the grotto of the Villa di Castello (see *Option 7*).

The vast hall on the right, formerly the courtroom, contains Donatello's *St George* (1416), a puzzled, uneasy figure, alert to some unseen danger, and the same sculptor's erotically charged *David* (1440), wearing not much more than an enigmatic smile. On the right-hand wall are the two trial panels made by Ghiberti and Brunelleschi, the winner and runner-up respectively in the competition of 1401 to find a designer for the Baptistry doors; both show the *Sacrifice of Isaac*.

The rest of this rich museum is a mixed bag covering everything

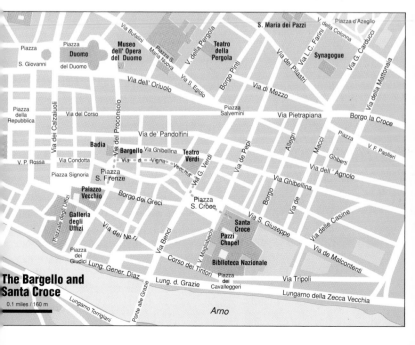

The Bargello and Santa Croce

0.1 miles / 160 m

Calcio festival, Piazza Santa Croce

from Islamic ceramics to coins and armour. Exploring at will you are bound to find something of interest; perhaps the 6th-century Lombardic jewellery or the rich Persian carpets on this floor, or the sculptures by Verrocchio on the floor above.

Leaving the Bargello, turn left and first left down Via della Vigna Vecchia. At the second turning right look for the **Bar Vivoli Gelateria** (Via Isola delle Stinche 7r, closed Monday), a tiny ice-cream parlour that attracts huge crowds for its imaginative concoctions. Newspaper clippings on the wall carry rave reviews proclaiming this the home of the 'best ice-cream in the world'.

From here it is a short walk down Via de' Lavatoi, then right, into the huge square fronting **Santa Croce** (Monday–Saturday 7am–12.30pm and 3–6.30pm; Sunday 3–6pm), the magnificent Gothic burial place of many famous Florentines. On the right-hand side of the entrance door, heading up the aisle, you will find Michelangelo's tomb, carved by Vasari, Dante's empty sarcophagus (he refused to return to the city that sent him into exile and is actually buried in Ravenna), and the graves of Machiavelli, Leonardo Bruni, the humanist, and the composer, Rossini.

The Bardi Chapel (to the right of the high altar) is covered in Giotto's frescos on the *Life of St Francis*, and the corridor on the right leads past the sacristy to the chapel containing Galileo's simple grave. The floor of the church is also covered in carved grave slabs.

Outside and to the left of the church is the entrance to the **Museo dell'Opera di Santa Croce** (Thursday–Tuesday, 10am–12.30pm and 2.30–6.30pm (but 3-5pm in winter), closed Wednesday). Here you will be charmed by the quiet serenity of the two cloisters and amused by some of the 19th-century tombs that line the cloister walk; this leads to the **Pazzi Chapel**, a supremely noble building of white walls and contrasting grey *pietra serena* pilasters, designed by Brunelleschi.

Home of 'the best ice cream in the world'

Option 2. Around Santissima Annunziata

Brunelleschi's Innocenti orphanage, Santissima Annunziata and the Archaeological Museum.

This morning tour takes in a clutch of little-visited museums and monuments in the north of the city. From Piazza del Duomo, head up Via dei Servi. The street is likely to be busy with traffic and the pavements crowded with Florentines heading for work, but do try to find a quiet doorway from which to admire some of Via dei Servi's imposing buildings.

At the first junction, note the **Palazzo Pucci** on the left, home of the Marchese Pucci and headquarters of his fashion empire. Further up on the left, at No 15, the **Palazzo Niccolini** (1550) is an appropriate headquarters for the Ministry of Public works – note the *sgraffito* decoration (designs scratched in plaster) and the huge overhanging roof sheltering an open loggia.

Via dei Servi leads into **Piazza della Santissima Annunziata**, one of the most beautiful squares in Florence, though cars and coaches detract from its visual harmony. In the centre of the square is an equestrian statue of Duke Ferdinand I, by Giambologna; it is partnered by two bronze fountains (by Tacca, 1608) featuring marine monsters and proving that the 20th century does not have a monopoly on bizarre fantasy creations.

On the right-hand side of the square is the gracious colonnade of the **Spedale degli Innocenti** built by Brunelleschi from 1419 and the very first classical loggia of its type. Here the elegant columns of grey *pietra serena* alternate harmoniously with Luca della Rob-

bia's blue and white terracotta roundels depicting a baby in swaddling clothes – the symbol of the Innocenti orphanage which lies behind. The orphanage, the first in the world (opened in 1444), is still in operation. It has a small **gallery** of pictures donated by wealthy patrons, including Ghirlandaio's radiant *Adoration* (open Monday–Saturday 9am–2pm, Sunday 8am–1pm, closed Wednesday, 3,000 lire).

Brunelleschi's portico was copied on the opposite side of the square, where it fronts the entrance to one of the best hotels in Florence, the Loggiata dei

Romantic city

Serviti, and on the north side, where it forms the entrance to the church of **Santissima Annunziata** (open daily 7am–12.30pm and 4–7pm, admission free). This contains some outstanding frescos, including Andrea del Sarto's *Birth of the Virgin*

The Chimera in the Museo Archeologico

(1514) and, in the adjacent Chiostro dei Morti (Cloister of the Dead), the same artist's *Holy Family*.

In the top right-hand corner of the square, at Via della Colonna 36, you will find the **Museo Archeologico**, the Archaeological Museum (open Tuesday–Saturday 9am–2pm, Sunday 9am–1pm, closed Monday, 6,000 lire). Prominence here is given to a rich collection of ancient Egyptian material which resulted from a joint French-Italian expedition of 1889; it includes superbly well-preserved clothing and wooden furniture as well as a complete 14th-century BC chariot. The real stars of the museum, however, are the Etruscan bronzes in Room XIV. The *Chimera* (5th century BC), part lion, part goat and part snake, was discovered in Arezzo in 1554 and was greatly admired by Renaissance bronze-casters, including Benvenuto Cellini, who was entrusted with its restoration.

Inside Santissima Annunziata

Masterpieces of Gothic and Renaissance sculpture in wood, bronze and marble.

The **Museo dell'Opera del Duomo** (Cathedral Works Museum) is one of Florence's best small museums and it has the merit of long opening hours, so you can pop in and see it whenever you have a spare moment – over lunch, perhaps, when much else is closed (open Monday–Saturday 9am–7.30pm in summer, 9am–6pm in winter, closed Sunday, 4,000 lire). If you want a coffee and a snack first, try the **Gran Caffe**, Piazza San Giovanni 1r, directly opposite the south doors of the Baptistry on Piazza del Duomo – a chic coffee bar with colourful fresco fragments on the wall.

Turn right out of the café and walk along the south flank of the Duomo, passing Giotto's campanile, and bearing left round the east end of the cathedral. Look for an archway on the right, with the bust of Duke Cosimo I above – No 9 Piazza del Duomo – and enter the courtyard of the museum. It was here, between 1501 and 1504, that Michelangelo carved his mighty statue of *David*. The courtyard is now decorated with baroque sculptures and Roman sarcophagi. The building that houses the museum was the office of the Cathedral Workshop, established in the 15th century to maintain the fabric of the cathedral and commission new works. Today it houses numerous sculptural works, principally from the cathedral exterior, brought indoors to protect them against pollution and weathering.

The first room contains displays on the construction of the cathedral dome and examples of the pulleys, capstans and winches used by 15th-century labourers. Another room contains sculptures intended for the cathedral facade, which didn't get completed until the 19th century. Most striking of the figures is Donatello's *St John the Evangelist*; compare this with Ciuffagni's *St Matthew* – clearly an attempt to imitate Donatello's style.

The mezzanine floor is devoted to a single work – Michelangelo's *Pietà*, begun around 1550 and originally intended for his own tomb. The tall hooded figure at the centre of the group is a self-portrait – Michelangelo cast himself as Nicodemus, the rich

Michelangelo's 'Pietà'

14th-century panel in the museum

man who donated his tomb for the burial of Christ. The rather stiff and inferior carving of Mary Magdalene, to the left, is by one of Michelangelo's pupils. The great master himself broke up the sculpture, dissatisfied with his work, and it survived only because a servant kept the pieces.

On the first floor are two superb *cantorie*, choir galleries, carved in marble and removed from the cathedral in the 17th century. Both depict young musicians in a joyous frenzy of dancing and cymbal-crashing. They were made by two of the leading artists of the day, Donatello and Luca della Robbia, between 1431 and 1438.

Discussing the next move

Here, too, you will find Donatello's powerful *Mary Magdalene*, a figure of penitence carved in wood, her features haggard from fasting and grief.

Beyond, a whole room is devoted to the panels that once adorned Giotto's campanile, some designed by Giotto, others by Andrea Pisano. Amongst other subjects, they depict various trades, showing in vivid detail what the workshop of a sculptor or artist would have looked like in the 14th century.

In the last room of the museum, Lorenzo Ghiberti's original bronze panels from the Paradise (east) door of the Baptistry are displayed – some are already here and others are still being restored. They provide an admirable opportunity for visitors to study in close-up the work that has come to stand as a symbol of the birth of the Renaissance.

The Room of the Parrots, Palazzo Davanzati

Option 4. The Palazzo Davanzati

Step inside this beautiful palace for a taste of life in Renaissance Florence before exploring nearby medieval alleys.

Start at the **Palazzo Davanzati**, Via Porta Rossa 13, also known as the **Museo dell'Antica Casa Fiorentina** (open Tuesday–Saturday 9am–2pm, Sunday 9am–1pm, closed Monday, 4,000 lire).

Look at the façade first; this dates to the mid-14th century and is a typical example of Tuscan pre-Renaissance architecture. You will see plenty of buildings like this in Siena and other Tuscan cities, but in Florence it is a rarity because of the huge amount of rebuilding that went on from the 15th century. A typical feature is the so-called depressed arch over the doors and windows. The coat of arms is that of the Davanzati family who owned the palace from 1518 until 1538. The open loggia that crowns the palace was added in the 16th century.

Inside is a very beautiful courtyard and an elegant stone staircase supported on flying arches. Note, too, the well to the right of the entrance with its pulley system enabling buckets of water to be lifted to each of the five floors of the palace – having a private water supply was a considerable luxury, since most Florentines were dependent on the water supplied by public fountains, which needed fetching and carrying by bucket.

The principal living-rooms lie on the first floor, the *piano nobile*, where you will find the gorgeously frescoed dining-room, known as the **Sala dei Papagalli** (Room of the Parrots) after the birds pictured in the borders. The bedchambers on the floors above have similar murals, notably the room on the second floor, which is decorated with scenes from the 13th-century French romance, the *Châtelaine de Vergy*. Though the contemporary furnishings in each room, consisting of beds, chests and stools, may look sparse, they

BENVENUTO CELLINI

represent a considerable degree of luxury for the time, as do the private bathrooms off each room, complete with toilets and terracotta waste pipes. The kitchen is located on the top floor, so that smoke and cooking smells would not permeate the living-rooms. Here, too, you will find a fascinating array of contemporary utensils, including equipment for kneading and shaping pasta.

As you leave the palace, look opposite and to the left to see the remains of a medieval tower-house, typical of an even earlier, medieval, style of architecture. Turn right and first right again, in Via Pellicheria, to reach another well-preserved group of medieval structures, the battlemented buildings of the **Palazzo di Parte Guelfa**. This dates to the 13th century and was aesthetically enhanced by Vasari, who built the external staircase in the 16th century. This palace once served as the headquarters of the Guelf party, one of the political factions whose feuding caused mayhem in the city during the 13th and 14th centuries.

Walk through the tunnel straight ahead and turn right in Via delle Terme (former site of the Roman baths) with its narrow medieval alleys leading off to the left. Take the second left, Via del Fiordaliso, noting the huge stone *sporti*, or brackets, of the building to the right, supporting the jettied-out upper storeys. Turn right, then first left into **Piazza del Limbo**, so called because the site was once used as a graveyard for unbaptised infants whose souls, according to the prevailing dogma, could not enter heaven and dwelled in Limbo. The church on the left, **Santi Apostoli**, is one of the oldest in the city, dating to around 1050.

Turn left in Borgo Sante Apostoli and cross the busy **Piazza di Santa Trinità** to the church of the same name (open daily 7am–noon and 4–7pm, admission free). Here the relative austerity of the 13th-century Gothic architecture contrasts with Ghirlandaio's stunningly colourful frescos and altarpiece of the **Sassetti Chapel**, to the right of the choir. The frescos (1483) illustrate the *Life of St Francis* and the altarpiece (1485) shows the *Nativity*. Other frescos depict scenes from classical writing and mythology set against a Florentine backdrop, suggesting that Renaissance Florence was conceived as being the new Rome.

Option 5. San Miniato al Monte

This somewhat strenuous walk to the jewel-like church of San Miniato and the Piazzale Michelangelo is rewarded by sweeping views down over the rooftops of Florence.

The lovely Romanesque church of San Miniato al Monte sits on a hill to the south of the city and Florentines head here for their Sunday afternoon walk. You can, of course, visit any day of the week, timing your walk to coincide with the church opening hours (daily 8am–noon and 2.30–7pm (6pm in winter), admission free).

From **Piazza della Signoria**, walk south through the courtyard of the Uffizi gallery to the Arno embankment and turn left. As you follow the river, look up to the right where you will see the green and white marble facade of San Miniato. The view across the Arno to this church was celebrated in E M Forster's novel, *A Room With a View* – the room concerned was located in the Pensione Simi (now the Jennings-Riccioli hotel). When you reach the first bridge, the Ponte alle Grazie, the hotel stands a little further up on the left.

Cross the bridge and take the third left, Via di San Miniato. This leads you through an arch in the 14th-century city wall, where you turn left in Via dei Bastioni.

Keep left and then look for a set of stone steps on the right which leads straight uphill, interrupted every so often by the main road, passing through leafy gardens. When the staircase stops, turn right along the road and look for a gate on the left leading into the **Giardino delle Rose**, or Rose Garden (open daily 9am–7pm, admission free). There is much more to see here than just roses and plant-lovers will delight in the colourful profusion. Follow the path through the garden and, at the exit gates, climb the steps to

In the Piazzale Michelangelo

Souvenirs

the right to reach the **Piazzale Michelangelo**. This viewpoint was laid out in the 19th century and the broad square is dotted with reproductions of Michelangelo's celebrated sculptures – not to mention scores of tour buses and numerous souvenir stalls. The views, though, are marvellous – this is where all those classic postcard pictures of the rooftops of Florence are taken from.

Turning your back on the Piazzale, head for the **Bar/Ristorante La Loggia**, housed in a 19th-century neo-classical building, where you may want to stop for lunch. If not, keep to the right of the restaurant, then take the flight of steps to the left which leads up to the church of San Salvatore. Follow the path to the right of this church, then take the left-most road towards an arch in the wall surrounding **San Miniato** and its conventual buildings. Catch your breath while admiring the views from the terrace in front of the church and studying its delicate facade, covered in geometric patterns of green and white marble.

The church was built on the site of the tomb of the city's first Christian martyr, St Minias. He was executed in AD250 during the anti-Christian purges of the Emperor Diocletian and his shrine was replaced by the present church in AD1018. Important features inside

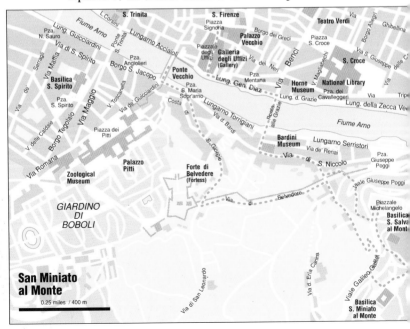

are the intarsia panels of the floor, now somewhat worn, depicting signs of the zodiac, and the numerous fragments of 11th- and 12th-century Byzantine-style frescos on the walls. To the left, behind an iron grille, is the splendid tomb of the Cardinal of Portugal who died on a visit to Florence in 1439. The mosaic in the apse, of 1297, shows **Christ, the Virgin and St Minias**.

With your back to the church facade, descend the stone staircase opposite, passing through the cemetery and noting the fine 19th-century sculptures marking some of the graves. Cross the road, continue down the next set of steps, cross the next

The view from Piazzale Michelangelo

road and bear right to find Via del Monte alle Croci on the left. Follow this winding road downhill until you return to the arch in the city wall.

A little café to the left (the **Fuori Porta**) has a quiet sunny terrace for enjoying coffee or ice-cream. You can now retrace your earlier steps to the city centre, or turn left to follow Via di Belvedere. This involves a steep uphill climb, following the foot of the city walls, until you reach Porta San Giorgio, built in 1260 and the city's oldest surviving gate.

Alongside the gate is an entrance to the **Forte Belvedere** (open daily 9am–8pm in summer, to 7pm in winter, admission free) which you can enter for more sweeping views of the city before descending through the Boboli Gardens (see *Day 3*). Alternatively, pass through the Porta San Giorgio and descend the quiet Costa San Giorgio, noting No 19 which stands on the site of Galileo's home. Where the road forks, take the left branch to reach Piazza Santa Felicità, just a few steps from the Ponte Vecchio and the north bank.

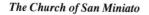

The Church of San Miniato

Option 6. Fiesole

Escape to the hills for a walk and lunch in the sleepy village that stands less than 4 miles/6km from the centre of Florence.

Fiesole is a favourite retreat for Florentines who find the air in this hilltop village fresher and cooler than in the valley bottom where their own city sits. Once, relations between Florence and Fiesole were not so comfortable. Fiesole predates Florence by some eight centuries; it was a major Etruscan city well before the Romans colonised the area and founded the town from which Florence grew. Thereafter Fiesole declined but remained an important trade competitor to Florence, with the rival towns constantly at war. Matters came to a head in 1125 when Florentine troops stormed Fiesole, winning an easy victory, and destroying all the buildings, save only for the cathedral.

Many a fine rural villa was built on the slopes leading up to Fiesole from the 15th century and these were rented by members of the city's Anglo-Florentine community (including the poets Robert and Elizabeth Barrett Browning) in the 19th century. You will see these villas from the bus as you approach Fiesole – take bus No 7 from **Santa Maria Novella** station, remembering to buy your ticket in advance from one of the ticket machines located on the pavement alongside the bus stop. The journey takes a matter of minutes and ends at the **Piazza Mino**, Fiesole's broad main square.

Cross the square to find the entrance to the **Teatro Romano** (open daily 9am–7pm in summer, 10am–4pm in winter, 5,000 lire).

This Roman amphitheatre, with a seating capacity of 3,000, is still used as the venue for the Estate Fiesolana arts festival held in July and August (see *Calendar of Events*).

It enjoys stunning views over the low, cypress-topped hills of

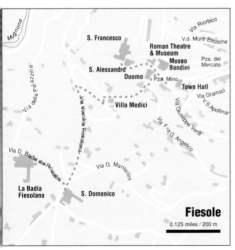

Fiesole
0.125 miles / 200 m

the rural Mugello region to the north. Surrounding the theatre are the jumbled remains of Etruscan and Roman temples and baths. The excellent **Museum Faesulanum**, within the same complex, displays archaeological finds from the Bronze Age to the 13th century.

Almost opposite the theatre entrance, in Via Dupre, the **Museo Bandini** has a collection of paintings, furniture, majolica and Byzantine carved ivories (open daily 10am–noon and 3–7pm in summer, 10am–12.30pm and 2.30–6pm in winter, 4,000 lire).

Back on the Piazza Mino, turn right to the rather forbidding and over-restored **Duomo** (cathedral). Look for Via San Francesco, the lane that climbs steeply from the cathedral facade. The views from here down over Florence can be enjoyed from lookout points or over a leisurely lunch from the terrace of the popular restaurant, **La Loggia degli Etruschi**.

Continue up to **Sant'Alessandro**, whose neo-classical facade hides a 6th-century basilica with re-used Roman columns of *cipollino* (onion-ring) marble. From here a path climbs upwards again to **San Francesco**, seated on the site of an Etruscan temple, with far-reaching views and a charming cloister. Retrace your steps to Piazza Mino and, if you have not eaten yet, take your pick from the numerous cafés and restaurants gathered around the square.

You can now return to Florence by bus, or walk part of the way, following the narrow Via Vecchia Fiesolana out of the square. You will pass the Villa Medici, built in 1458, a favourite retreat of Lorenzo de'Medici and the childhood home of Iris Origo, the Anglo-American author of *The Merchant of Prato*.

The next stop after ½ a mile (1km) is the **convent of San Domenico** where you can see Fra Angelico's *Madonna with Angels* (1430) in the church and his *Crucifixion* (1430) in the Chapter House. Opposite

Mixed facade of the Badia Fiesolana

the church, Via della Badia leads down to the **Badia Fiesolana**, the church that served as Fiesole's cathedral until 1058. Its original Romanesque facade, framed by the rough, unfinished stonework of the enlarged 15th-century church, is a delicate work of inlaid marble. There is another magnificient view over Florence from the terrace in front of the church. Return to the convent of San Domenico where there is a stop for the No 7 bus back to Florence.

A visit to two Medici villas with fine gardens in the northern suburbs of the city.

This tour is a must for garden-lovers – but don't expect colourful herbaceous borders: the two gardens we will visit today were laid out in the formal Italian style in the 16th century, and are of great historical interest. They are open all day, every day except Monday, and can be enjoyed in all seasons. The garden of the Villa della Petreia is backed by extensive woodland, perfect for picnicking.

Take bus 28A, B or C from the stop to the extreme right of the **Santa Maria Novella** bus station. Buses leave every 15 minutes or so and tickets can be bought from the machine by the bus-stop.

Knowing where to get off the bus is going to be the most challenging part of this tour – befriend someone on the bus, if possible, and ask them to tell you where to get off for the Villa Medicea della Petreia. Alternatively, keep an eye on the street signs – the bus heads north to the suburb of Rifredi, then follows the railway track along the long Via Reginaldo Giuliani. After about 15 minutes you will pass a power station on the right just before Via

Lurking figure, Villa di Castello

Reginaldo Giuliani narrows down to a single lane. Count the house numbers on the right – you want to get out at the request stop outside house No 424.

From there, walk back to house No 292 and turn left up the narrow Via della Petreia. About ⅓ mile/0.5km up the lane you will pass the Villa Corsini, with its cream-coloured baroque facade and a plaque recording that Robert Dudley died here on September 6, 1649. Dudley, the illegitimate son of the Earl of Leicester (Queen Elizabeth I's favourite) was the leading marine engineer of his age and was employed by Cosimo I to build the harbour at Livorno, Tuscany's principal port.

The **Villa della Petreia** is another ⅔ mile/1km up from here (open Tuesday–Saturday 9am–7.30pm (but closing earlier in winter), Sunday 9am–1.30pm, closed Monday, admission free).

Enter the gate and take the first entrance in the wall on the right, passing into the garden that fronts the villa, laid out with low box hedges enclosing flower beds. Take the central path up steps and past a large fish tank to the terrace in front of the villa. From here the scroll work and geometric patterning of the box parterre can best be appreciated. There is a good view from here

Villa della Petreia

left to the dome of Florence cathedral, straight ahead to the new industrial suburb of Firenze Nuova and right to the city's Peretola airport.

Tours of the villa itself are only given to groups of 10, so you may have to wait and team up with other visitors (then press the bell to the right of the entrance). The main sight is the central hallway, covered in frescos on the history of the Medici. The villa itself was built in 1575 for Grand Duke Ferdinand I, on the site of an earlier fortress, whose tower is still preserved. During the 19th century it was the favourite residence of the King of Italy, Victor Emmanuel II and it was he who had the tree house built in the huge (and now dead) ilex oak to the left of the villa facade.

To the right of the villa, a gate in the wall leads to a large park full of ilex and cypress trees, dense enough to be cool even in the heat of summer and threaded with little streams. This juxtaposition of the very formal garden with wild and mysterious woodland was a favourite device of Italian gardeners.

From the Villa della Petreia, return downhill to the Villa Corsini and turn right, down Via di Castello. Follow this road, ignoring all side turnings, and you will find the **Villa di Castello** on the right after ⅓ mile/0.5km (open Tuesday–Sunday 9am–7.30pm (but closing earlier in winter), closed Monday, admission free).

Turn left at the rear of the villa (not open to the public) to reach the formal garden, laid out for Duke Cosimo I in 1541 and once regarded as the supreme example of Renaissance gardening – for the Grand Tourists of the 18th and 19th century, this was a compulsory sight. It now lacks some of the features that made it famous – at the back of the garden, the shell-encrusted **Grotta degli Animali** (1579) was once filled with the delightful bronze birds of Giambologna, since moved to the Bargello Museum (see *Option 1*). Even so, the geometric beds, outlined in box, and the rows of huge terracotta pots containing citrus trees and bougainvillaea are very striking and, viewed from the upper terrace, resemble a vast patterned carpet.

Once again, the ordered formality of the parterre contrasts with the wilder woodland above, where the shivering figure of Appennino (by Ammanati) rises from a pool.

To return to Florence, exit from the villa and walk down the avenue directly opposite. Cross Via Peginalio Giuliani and continue down Via Fiulio Bechi. Cross the next road, Via Sestesi, and look for the bus-stop a short way down on the right.

Flow with the crowds on an early evening stroll around the city, taking in the principal shops.

The *passeggiata*, or evening promenade, is a traditional feature of northern Italian life. From about 6pm, as people finish their work for the day, everyone pours out onto the central streets of Florence. There they stroll arm-in-arm to do some last-minute shopping, stopping to greet old friends and gossip, or they stand in conspiratorial groups to discuss appropriate issues in business, politics or the latest *cause célèbre*.

Watching other people is all part of the fun and in Florence – where locals and foreign visitors intermingle – it is not hard to spot the true Florentines because of the way they dress; looking good (*fare bella figura*) is a matter in which they take pride. As you join the crowds we will note some of the main shops of central Florence, whose attractive window-displays act as punctuation marks along the way – you may be tempted to fit yourself out with a set of smart new clothes so as to look as much as possible like an honorary Florentine.

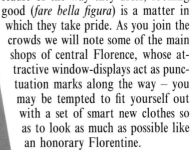

Ready for a promenade

Start in **Piazza del Duomo** and head south down Via Calzaiuoli. The first shop on the right, **Armando Poggi** (103r), stocks kitchenware and china, from classic designs to ultra-modern; this is the place where wealthy young Florentines place their wedding lists.

Further down, at **Migone** (85r), you can buy little hand-painted boxes and fill them with a selection of chocolates, bonbons, marzipan fruits or sweet biscuits. A little way down on the left, **Ceramiche Calzaiuoli** (80r) is packed to the ceiling with reproduction Renaissance majolica and more modern pieces, everything from small tiles to huge jars and bowls.

Also on the left, **Coin** (56r) is a fashionable galleria, selling chic own-label clothing that does not cost the earth. By contrast **Beltrami** (both sides of the street, 44r and 31r) is at the high-cost end of the fashion market. From these two shops Beltrami first began selling the shoes, clothing and leather goods that are now renowned throughout Italy.

Ice-creams coming up: **Perche Noi** (meaning 'Why Not?') is one of the oldest and best *gelati* makers in the city; the little shop is on the left, just after Beltrami, at Via dei Tavolini 19r. On the right, just at the entrance to Piazza della Signoria, is **Pineider** (13r); stop to admire the hand-printed stationery, albums, prints and leather briefcases. Well-bred Italians, heads of state and Hollywood film stars have their personalised stationery printed here. This city is well-known for its paper products.

Turn right in Via Caccherec-cia, past the **Erboristeria** (Herbalist) at No 9r, with its frescoed and beamed interior. Turn left in Via Por Santa Maria and follow the crowds to Ponte Vecchio. Apart from the numerous jewellers' shops, you may well find buskers and street traders on the bridge (keeping a wary eye out for the police). Be wary yourself of any bargains that seem too good to be true.

The crowd pushes on south down Via Guicciardini. Follow the flow and look out for **Del Secco** (20r) selling lace and hand-embroidered linen, and **Giulio Giannini e Figlio** (37r) where you can buy marbled papers, notepads, albums and paper sculpture. In Piazza dei Pitti, **Pitti Mosaici** (16r) keeps alive the ancient art of making tables with *trompe-l'oeuil* designs out of inlaid marble and semi-precious stones; you can also buy more portable items, such as

Florence is famous for its marbled paper

jewellery. A little way beyond this, **Frieze of Papier Mâché** (10r) makes everything from traditional carnival masks to enormous painted murals.

Turn back and swim against the flow of human bodies to reach Piazza della Signoria. Take a seat and a well-earned rest at **Rivoire**, the café with the best view of the square. Watch the buskers, the crowds, the pigeons and the horse-drawn carriages over a rich cup of iced chocolate and, if you have any money left, take away a tiny box of Rivoire's handmade chocolates as a souvenir.

Option 9. Excursion to Pisa

Visit the world-famous Leaning Tower, the cathedral, Baptistry and Camposanto on a day trip from Florence.

Many visitors to Florence arrive and depart from Pisa's Galileo Galilei airport, but never find time to visit Pisa itself. This is a pity, since Pisa is very easy to reach from Florence and its sights are memorable. Trains for Pisa depart from **Santa Maria Novella** station in Florence every hour, on the hour, every day of the week and the fare is very cheap.

The train follows the Arno valley downstream, calling first at the industrial town of Empoli, before arriving at Pisa Centrale station after 53 minutes. Alight here and exit the station, heading straight up Viale Gramsci, crossing the busy Piazza Vittoria Emanuele and continuing up Corso Italia.

This brings you to the banks of the Arno river, much wider here than in Florence and bridged by the Ponte di Mezzo. Cross to Piazza Garibaldi and walk up the arcaded Borgo Stretto, Pisa's animated main shopping street. Take the first left, Via Dini, to reach the **Piazza dei Cavalieri**.

This square is dominated by the Palazzo della Carovana, built by Vasari in 1562 and covered in black and white *sgraffito* decoration. The palazzo stands on the site of Pisa's original town hall, demolished in 1509 to symbolise the subjugation of Pisa after the city had been defeated by the Florentines.

A large and domineering statue of Duke Cosimo I stands in front of the palace. To the right of the palace is the church of Santo Stefano which contains war trophies captured by the crusading *cavalieri* (knights) of St Stephen in battles with the Turks. To the left is the grim Torre Gualandi, known as the Tower of Hunger, where Count Ugolino, along with all his sons and grandsons, was walled up and starved to death in 1288 for allegedly betraying Pisa to the Genoese – the story is told in Dante's *Inferno* (Canto XXXIII) and Shelley's poem, *The Tower of Famine*.

Pass under the arch beneath the clock tower of the Palazzo dell'Orologia, to the left, and take the right-hand street, Via Martiri. This bends left to join Via San Giuseppe, which leads to the **Campo dei Miracoli** (Field of Miracles) where the bizarre ensemble of Pisa's Leaning Tower, cathedral and Baptistry is revealed.

The Duomo's facade dates from 1063

No matter how many photographs you may have seen, nothing prepares you for the impact of these extraordinary buildings seen at first hand. Pisa was a thriving port until the mouth of the River Arno silted up, and the city had extensive trade contacts with Spain and North Africa during the 12th and 13th centuries – hence the Moorish influence on the architecture of these idiosyncratic buildings, evident in the marble arabesque patterns that cover the walls of the cathedral and the bristling, minaret-like pinnacles of the Baptistry. All of the buildings tilt – not just the Leaning Tower; hence the effect of vertigo you will experience if you look too long.

The **Leaning Tower**, begun in 1173, started to tilt during the early stages of construction, when it was only 35-ft (10.5-metre) high (some people say the Pisans deliberately built it this way so as to ensure a healthy income from tourism). Completed in 1350, the tower has continued to slide, so that now, 180-ft (54.5-metre) high, it leans 15ft (4.5 metre) from the perpendicular. It is likely that the tower will be supported by scaffolding when you visit: to prevent further subsidence, a 300 billion lire programme of underpinning began in 1991 that will take several years to complete.

The **Duomo** (cathedral) alongside is as interesting for its exterior as its interior. It was begun in 1063 and the facade is covered in rising tiers of colonnades, typical of the distinctive Pisan Romanesque style. The bronze doors below these colonnades date to 1602 and illustrate biblical scenes. The cathedral is entered through the south transept which also has important Romanesque bronze doors, designed by Bonnano da Pisa in 1180 and illustrating scenes from the *Life of Christ*.

Fire devastated the interior in 1595 but spared Cimabue's mosaic of *Christ in Majesty* (1302) in the vault of the apse and Giovanni Pisano's outstanding pulpit carved with New Testament scenes. The work of the father-and-son team, Nicola and Giovanni Pisano, transcends art historical categories. Though working in the 13th century, when Gothic was the predominant style, their output anticipates the best Renaissance sculpture of the next century. You will see more of it in the Baptistry, which was designed and completed by the Pisani in 1284 and contains Nicola Pisano's fine pulpit, carved with animated scenes from the *Life of Christ*.

Vasari tells us that the Pisani were influenced by the carvings on the Roman sarcophagi that are to be found in the **Camposanto** (Holy Field) cemetery that lies to the north of the cathedral, enclosed by marble walls. This was begun in 1278, and shiploads of soil were brought back from the Holy Land, along with the sarcophagi, in Pisan ships to add sanctity to the burial ground. The cloister walls surrounding the cemetery were once gloriously frescoed, but they were seriously damaged when a stray Allied bomb hit the cemetery in 1944. Even so, fragments remain of a lively *Last Judgment* by an unknown 14th-century artist.

On the opposite side of the Campo dei Miracoli is the **Museo delle Sinopie**, to which the remaining frescos of the Camposanto have been removed. Many of them consist of nothing more than the *sinopie*, preliminary designs sketched into the plaster undercoat to guide the artist during the final stage – painting the finished fresco on to the moist final coat of plaster. Perhaps more interesting is the **Museo dell'Opera del Duomo** on the corner of the Piazza del Duomo nearest to the Leaning Tower. This contains numerous works of art, including Giovanni Pisano's exquisite *Virgin and Child* carved in ivory, and there is an unusual view of the Leaning Tower from the museum courtyard.

From Piazza del Duomo, take Via Roma southwards, passing the Orto Botanica (Botanical Garden) until you reach the Arno embankment. Turn right along Lungarno Simonelli and cross the next bridge. Turn left to reach the church of **San Paolo a Ripa d'Arno**, with another splendid Pisan Romanesque facade. Further down the Arno embankment is the extraordinary church of **Santa Maria della Spina**, covered in prickly pinnacles and niches containing statues of the Virgin, Christ and the Apostles. This 14th-century Gothic church was built to house a thorn from the Crown of Thorns, a theme picked up in the bristling exterior architecture.

A right turn here will take you down Via Sant'Antonio and back to Pisa Centrale station, from where hourly trains depart for Florence at 46 minutes past the hour.

Santa Maria della Spina

Shopping

Some visitors come to Florence simply to shop – never mind the monuments. To be this indulgent you have to be affluent, however, since even a casual suit or pair of shoes is going to cost 500,000 lire. For those of lesser means, window-shopping can be almost as much fun, and there are genuine bargains to be found if you search diligently enough, especially in the big street markets around San Lorenzo and the Mercato Nuovo.

High fashion in Via de' Tornabuoni

Although Milan claims to be the world capital of *haute couture*, Florence has its fair share of homegrown designers of international repute. Nearly all have their outlets at the southern end of Via de' Tornabuoni. The exception is Emilio Pucci, famous for his sexy underwear and for inventing the trouser suit (known as palazzo pyjamas when trouser suits were all the rage as evening wear in the 1960s). The Marchese Pucci is fortunate enough to live in an ancestral palace, designed by Ammanati, at Via de' Pucci 6; here you will find the Pucci boutique, while the shop around the corner (Via Ricasoli 20r) sells Chianti Classico wines, Vinsanto and olive oil from the Pucci estates.

A tour of Via de'Tornabuoni should start on the eastern (even-numbered) side of the road. **Ugolini** (20-22r) sells gloves that are almost softer than skin, as worn by many members of the European nobility. At **Bijoux Casciou** (32r) the speciality is costume jewellery that looks like the real thing – and costs nearly as much.

Stationery for sale

Textiles at Casa dei Tessuti

At the bottom of the street (16r), in the 13th-century Palazzo Spini-Ferroni, is the boutique of **Salvatore Ferragamo** who, whilst working in Hollywood, became known as the 'shoemaker to the stars'. The family-run firm now sells clothing, luggage and relatively inexpensive silk scarves and ties, as well as the famous footwear.

Across on the west side of the road are rival shoemakers, **Casadei** (33r) and **Tanino Crisci** (43-45r). Then comes **Valentino** (67r); the jeweller **Mario Buccellati** (72r) and, last of all, the flagship store of **Gucci**, the designer whose products have spawned many millions of fakes.

The next street left, Via della Vigna Nuova, is now almost an extension of Via de' Tornabuoni. Here you will find brightly coloured fashions at **Enrico Coveri** (27-29r) and **Naj Oleari** (35r). Equally fun are the woven baskets, hats, furniture and sculptures at **Emilio Paoli** (26r). **Giorgio Armani** is a little further down (51r) and if, by now, you have had enough of clothes, go and see the period photographs on show at **Alinari** (46-48r) or the pens, pencils, Filofaxes and executive toys on sale at **&C** (82r).

Food, fashion and fabrics in the city centre

Just to the east of Piazza del Duomo, at Via dei Vecchietta 28r, is the **Old England Stores**, a long narrow shop lined with glass-fronted cabinets selling everything from breakfast cereals and Fortnum & Mason marmalade to cashmeres and tweed. Its existence bears witness to the fact that some Florentines hold certain British products in high regard – but it is also surprising how many British holidaymakers come here to buy the things they miss from home.

Heading east towards Piazza del Duomo, do not miss **Casa dei Tessuti** at Via de' Pecori 20-24r; this textile shop is piled to the ceiling with costly antique-style fabrics, rich enough to grace a Renaissance palace.

By contrast, **Max Mara** opposite (23r) is full of bold but stylishly tailored modern clothes. Turn right down Via Roma for **Luisa** (71r), a large boutique that stocks clothes designed by the likes of Issey Miyake, Comme des Garçons, Jean-Paul Gaultier, along with many others. **Eredi Chianini** opposite (18-22r) is a very masculine shop, selling everything from jeans and aftershave to silk underwear and suits.

Further down, **Gilli**, on the right (3r) is renowned for its handmade chocolates and perfect pastries. If you take coffee in the pavement café fronting Piazza della Repubblica, or in the wood-pan-

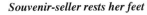

elled interior, you will be served by smart waiters in evening dress. Nearby, on the opposite left-hand side of the piazza, is the UPIM department store, a good place to shop if you cannot afford the rather high boutique prices.

Heading down Via Calimala, you will soon come to the crowded **Mercato Nuovo**, built in 1547 and packed with stalls selling leather goods, lace, costume jewellery, baskets and T-shirts. You may find some cheap and joky souvenirs here – a plastic illuminated model of Michelangelo's *David* perhaps?

Alternatively, look for inexpensive soaps, pot pourri, perfumes and fragrances at the **Erboristeria della Antica Farmacia del Cinghiale** (Via Calimala 4r) alongside the market.

Going for Gold

Jewellers have been operating from the Ponte Vecchio since the 16th century. Unfortunately, much of what is sold on the bridge today is mass-produced in factories elsewhere and geared to the (affluent) tourist's desire for an appropriate souvenir, so expect to

see a lot of charms and trinkets. For the more discerning, following below is a guide to the more interesting and creative jewellers on the bridge.

Bijoux Cascio is on the embankment just before the bridge (Via Por Santa Maria 1r) and proves that not

Jewellery for sale on Ponte Vecc

everything that glistens here is made of solid gold: this shop sells good chunky (gold-plated) modern jewellery at affordable prices.

Going up the left-hand side of the bridge, look for the glittering display in the window of **Ristori** (1-3r); if you need to ask the price, this shop is probably not for you. **U. Gherardi** (5r) is cheaper and specialises in coral and cultured pearls. **Piccini** (23r) is one of the more imaginative jewellers on the bridge but, if you prefer something more classic, it also sells antique pieces.

On the opposite side of the bridge, you may see crowds outside **Cassetti** (52r), a shop whose contemporary designs attract admiring Florentines, as well as visitors with money and taste.

Melli (44-46r) is worth looking at for something different; it sells only antique pieces – not just jewellery, but also silver snuff boxes, candlesticks, jugs and plates. Finally, **Rajola** (24r) is another affordable jeweller selling gold-plated pieces, set with semi-precious stones, plus elegant watches.

Tempting pastries

Food and drink

These shops are not on the beaten track but are the best in their class and worth seeking out. **Alessi**, Via dell' Oche 29r, sells the widest selection of chocolates, biscuits, Tuscan honey and jams, wines and spirits that you will find in Florence. The drinks section alone is a delightful showcase for local wines, spirits and liqueurs; here you can still buy traditional straw-wrapped flasks of Chianti, and the *grappa vecchia* produced by Jacopo Poli is worth buying just for the elegance of the bottle designs.

If you have time, turn right out of Alessi, down to the end of Via dell' Oche, to find more gastronomic treats at **Pegna** (Via della Studio 28r) – the place to buy olive oil, balsamic vinegar, sun-dried tomatoes, dried mushrooms and bottled *antipasti*.

Marbled paper

For marbled papers, a Florentine speciality, the best selection and

keenest prices are to be found at **Bottega Artigiana del Libro**, Lungarno Corsini 40r. Here you can buy sheets of paper, albums, notebooks, carnival masks and paper formed into delicate origami peacocks and flowers. While you are here do not miss **P. Bazzanti**, almost next door at 46r. This art gallery stocks bronze and marble reproductions of many Florentine statues – just the place to buy a nymph or deity for the garden.

A Ponte Vecchio to take home

Eating

You can eat very well and cheaply in Florence on pizza and pasta, or on a simple diet put together from the offerings of street markets or an *alimentare* (grocer). On some occasions absolutely nothing can beat a picnic of bread (*pane*), plump black olives (*olive*), tomatoes (*pomodore*), sheep's cheese (*pecorino*), Tuscan ham (*prosciutto*) and fruits such as figs, apricots or peaches (*fichi, albicocche, pesce*). Such a meal can be enjoyed in any number of enchanting settings – in a tree-shaded corner of the Boboli Gardens, for example, or in the ancient Roman theatre at Fiesole with its sweeping views over the gentle green hills of the Mugello.

Other occasions and other moods demand a full-blown meal in the Italian style, preferably *al fresco*, in a restaurant with a garden, since eating out in Italy is as much a social event as a gourmet experience. Everybody should try the Florentine speciality, *bistecca alla fiorentina*, at least once, despite the cost (the price on the menu is per unit (*etto*) of 100 grammes of raw meat and you will probably regret it if you do not order at least a half kilo – just over 1lb – per person). You can ask for it to be cooked rare (*al sangue*) or well-done (*ben cotta*). The result is a tender, juicy, rib steak, from cattle raised in the Val di Chiana, grilled over charcoal, fragrant with herbs and served with chunks of lemon; the taste is quite unlike any steak you will have eaten before.

Basic rules

If you decide to eat in a *ristorante* or a *trattoria* you will be expected to order a first course (*prima*) of pasta, rice (*risotto*) or soup (*minestra*), followed by a main course (*secondo*) of meat or fish. This is served without accompaniment; if you want salad (*insalata*) or vegetables, you will have to order additional side dishes

(*contorni*). The meal finishes with either fruit (*frutta*), cheese (*formaggio*), dessert (*dolci*) or ice-cream (*gelato*), followed by a coffee (*caffe* – invariably an *espresso*, unless you request otherwise). No meal would be complete unless partnered by the fruity red wines of Chianti (if you prefer white, try Vernaccio di San Gimignano), while for a final *digestive*, try Vinsanto, a sweet but complex dessert wine, golden in colour, often accompanied by little almond biscuits (*biscotti di Prato*) which are dipped into the wine; priests are said to be very fond of it, hence the name (literally 'Holy Wine').

Prices

The price categories quoted below are based on the average cost of a three-course meal for two, including cover and service charges, but excluding the cost of drink: *$* = up to 80,000 lire, *$$* = 80-140,000 lire, *$$$* = more than 140,000 lire.

Restaurants

ACQUA AL DUE
Via della Vigna Vecchia 40r
Tel: 284170
A good place to begin an acquaintance with Tuscan food, since this restaurant specialises in *assaggio*, a succession of different little dishes which enables you to taste a great range of *antipasti*, followed by a series of different pastas and sauces.

You can also sample a variety of desserts. Closed Monday; reservations advised. *$*

ANGIOLINO
Via Santo Spirito 36
Tel: 298976
The waiters are somewhat brusque (or at least pretend to be, to the delight of regulars) but the food is good, relatively cheap and authentic. Closed Sunday and Monday. *$*

Well-fed at Il Latine – see page 74

ANTICO FATTORE
Via Lambertesca 1r
Tel: 238 1215
Food for both body and mind; pasta in ample proportions in this haunt of the literati; tripe cooked with tomatoes is also a speciality. Closed Sunday, Monday and August. *$*

IL BARONE DI PORTA ROMANA
Piazza Santo Spirito 6
Tel: 210437
Rustic-style trattoria/pizzeria with outdoor dining in the leafy square in summer. A wide selection of pizzas cooked authentically in a wood-fired oven. Closed Sunday and Monday lunch. *$*

BUCA DELL'ORAFO
Volta dei Girolami 228r
Tel: 213619
Tiny but spirited cellar-restaurant by the Ponte Vecchio serving good-value *bistecca* and pasta. Closed Sunday lunch. *$$*

BUCA LAPI
Via del Trebbio 1r
Tel: 213768
In the cellar of the Palazzo Antino regarded as serving the best *bistec alla Fiorentina* in town, plus an exce lent range of local wines. Closed Su day. *$$*

CANTINETTA ANTINORI
Piazza Antinori 3
Tel: 292234
A showcase for the wines and oth products of the Antinori family, o of Tuscany's oldest and most respect wine-makers. Light snacks of del cious *crostini* (appetisers on toast bread) or full meals, plus the amb ence of an 15th-century palazz Closed Saturday, Sunday, August a public holidays. Reservations advise *$$*

LA CAPANNINA DI SANTE
Piazza Ravenna
Tel: 688345
Mainly fish, absolutely fresh. Try t *spaghetti di mare* (with seafood) for real feast. Closed Sunday, Mond lunch and August. *$$*

L CAVALLINO
Via delle Farine 6r
Tel: 215818
Though the entrance is on a side street, there is an outdoor dining area in Piazza della Signoria, a romantic place to eat, with a view of the Palazzo Vecchio. Genuine Tuscan food and a good choice for a Sunday, when many other restaurants are closed. Closed Tuesday evening.

CIBREO
Via dei Macci 118r
Tel: 234 1100
Simple décor and authentic Tuscan cuisine from elemental cold tripe salad to boned leg of lamb stuffed with artichoke – but no pasta dishes. You pay lower prices for much the same menu if you go round the corner and sit in the no-frills *trattoria* section at the back, entered from Piazza Ghiberti 35r. Closed Sunday, Monday and August. *$$*

COCO LEZZONE
Via del Parioncino 26
Tel: 287178
Crowded and chaotic restaurant in which you can sample real Tuscan peasant dishes such as *pappa al pomodoro* (bread, tomato and basil soup), *ribollita* (bread, beans and cabbage soup), Florentine-style tripe in tomato sauce and herb-flavoured roast pork. Closed Sunday, Tuesday evening and August. *$*

DA NOI
Via Fiesolana 46r
Tel: 242917
Intimate restaurant serving creative variations on a Tuscan theme – the sort of dishes that foodies rave about. Dinner only, closed Sunday, Monday, August and Christmas; reservations essential. *$$$*

ENOTECA PINCHIORRI
Via Ghibellina 87
Tel: 242777
Another gourmet paradise, garlanded with awards and hailed by some as one of the best restaurants in Europe, scorned, by others, as pretentious, over-priced and over-rated. Make up your own mind if you are wealthy enough. Traditional Tuscan dishes, outstanding wine-list and courtyard for summer dining. Closed Sunday, Monday lunch and August; reservations essential – best to book at least a week in advance. *$$$*

LE FONTICINE
Via Nazionale 78
Tel: 282106
Popular and atmospheric restaurant serving perfect pasta and juicy *bistecca*. Closed Monday and August. *$$*

Service at Harry's Bar

HARRY'S BAR
Lungarno Vespucci 22r
Tel: 239 6700
An entertaining place modelled on the original Harry's Bar in Venice, made famous by Hemingway. The cocktail bartender is a real showman. The restaurant serves good beefburgers and American-influenced Italian food. Closed Sunday. *$$*

I Che C'e C'e
Via Magalotti 11r
Tel: 216589
The name means 'What there is, there is', but this does not mean a lack of choice or a 'take it or leave it attitude'. The range of *crostini* (appetisers on toast), and the buffet of *antipasti* is superb and the daily specials are always unusual. The restaurant has many regulars and a friendly atmosphere. Closed Monday. *$*

A taste of Tuscany

Il Latine
Via del Palchetti 6r
Tel: 210916
Sprawling noisy restaurant with communal tables. Expect to queue, but not for too long as the turnover is fast. The reward for this discomfort is good, filling Tuscan food at very reasonable prices and the chance to make some new friends. Closed Monday, Tuesday lunch, late July to early August and Christmas. *$*

Otelo
Via degli Orti Oricellari 36r
Tel: 215819
A few steps from the railway statio serving classical Tuscan cuisine a humbler dishes. Closed Tuesday. *$$*

Sabatini
Via Panzani 41
Tel: 211559
Sober, old-fashioned setting for restaurant that has gained an inte national reputation for polished se vice and traditional Tuscan dishe try *pappardelle alla lepre* or *al cinghiale* (homemade pasta with wi hare or wild boar sauce) and an thing containing the magic wor *funghi* (wild mushrooms) or *aspara* (asparagus). Closed Monday in wi ter; reservations advised. *$$$*

Sostanza
Via del Porcellana 25r
Tel: 212691
Long-established *trattoria* (founde 1869), very plain and down-to-ear but patronised by famous guests fro Ezra Pound to Ronald Reagan (in h acting days). Equally famous is t speciality *petto di pollo al burr* chicken breast in butter. Closed Sa urday and Sunday. *$$*

Nightlife

The nightlife of Florence is relatively low-key and civilised. Florentines do not, on the whole, burn the night away in a frenetic trawl from one club or discotheque to another. Discos exist (barely tolerated by the local authority) but most Florentines prefer a leisurely meal and a stroll round their city in the cool of the night.

The tourist authority (APT) puts out a monthly poster – the Calendario delle Manifestazione (Calendar of Events) – which is displayed in most hotels; this is not a comprehensive guide, but it does list all the major events and your hotel concierge may well be willing to phone and book tickets (there is a central box-office at Via della Pergola 10; tel: 243361).

Alternatively, call at the tourist information office at Via Cavour 1r (next door to the Palazzo Medici-Riccardi); here there is a noticeboard displaying details of all the events of the day that can be enjoyed by English-speaking visitors, covering everything from films to jazz, rock and classical concerts, opera, dance and theatre. The staff will also help with bookings.

Night-time on the Arno at the Ponte alle Grazie

Bars & Clubs

LA DOLCE VITA
Piazza del Carmine 6
Tel: 284595
Very fashionable late-night bar decorated in post-modernist style and hung with the work of local artists and photographers. Live music on Thursdays from 11pm when the crowds spill out into the piazza. Closed Sunday.

FIDDLER'S ELBOW
Piazza Santa Maria Novella 7r
Tel: 216056
Straight out of James Joyce's Dublin, an Irish bar with real character (and real characters in the bar) serving Guinness and other imported beers.

GUIBBE ROSSE
Piazza della Repubblica 13r
Tel: 212280
Named after the red jackets of the waiters, this former haunt of artists and intellectuals is still a fine place to enjoy drinks, snacks and ice-cream whilst watching the busy nightlife of the square.

JAZZ CLUB
Via Nuova dei Caccini 3
Tel: 247 9700
Live jazz and a good range of beer

LOGGIA TORNAQUINCI
Via de'Tornabuoni 6
Tel: 219148
Sophisticated late-night piano ba Open from 10pm. Closed Mo day–Wednesday.

Pizza gossip

PASZKOWSKI
Piazza della Repubblica 6
Tel: 210236
Very grand piano bar (sometimes there is a small orchestra as well) playing light music and popular melodies; very popular with those old enough to remember when the songs were new. Closed Monday.

RIFLISSI D'EPOCHA
Via de' Renai 13r
Stylish basement club specialising in jazz and blues, with a video bar serving beer and cocktails. Open 8.30pm–6am. Entry free.

RIVOIRE
Piazza della Signoria 5r
Tel: 214412
The café with the best views of the Palazzo Vecchio. The place to while away a romantic moonlit evening over wine; cocktails, ice-cream or delicious pastries. Closed Monday and the last two weeks in January.

Cinema

ASTRO
Piazza San Simone (Via Isola delle Stinche)
English-language films every night except Monday.

Discos

CAPITALE
Via del Fosso Macinante 2-4
Tel: 356723
Dancing out of doors. Relaxed atmosphere. From 10pm.

ROCK CAFE
Borgo degli Albizi 66r
Tel: 244662
Live music plus disco. From 10pm.

SPACE ELECTRONIC
Via Palazzuolo 37
Tel: 293082
Huge ultra-modern disco where the in-crowd is entertained by videos, lasers, light shows and a giant spaceship that wanders around the dance floor. From 9.30pm. Closed Monday.

TENAX
Via Pratese 47
Tel: 37050
Occasional live acts from international stars. Mainly rock and new wave. The leading club for arty, fashionable Florentines. From 10pm.

YAB YUM
Via dei Sasseti 5
Tel: 282018
Fashionable and central, set in a vast basement, but still crowded. From 11pm. Closed Monday, Wednesday, July and August.

Calendar of Special Events

JANUARY – APRIL

Music-lovers should check listings magazines to see what is on at the Teatro Pergola, Via della Pergola 12 (Tel: 247 9651); during the first three months of the year the Amici della Musica (Friends of Music) organise a programme of chamber concerts.

25 March: the normally quiet Piazza delle Santissima Annunziata comes alive to the sounds of excited children celebrating the feast of the Annunciation.

Easter: the **Scoppio del Carro** (Explosion of the Cart) takes place in the Piazza del Duomo and ostensibly celebrates the Resurrection, though pre-Christian fertility rites may underlie the custom. Crowds gather in the piazza to watch an 18th-century painted cart, in the shape of a tower, being drawn by white oxen to the cathedral doors. If all goes well, a dove-shaped rocket swoops from the high altar through the cathedral doors and ignites the fireworks hidden in the carriage. The size and success of the conflagration serves as an omen that indicates the likely outcome of that year's harvest.

MAY – JULY

Maggio Musicale (Musical May), t[he] city's major arts festival, is no long[er] confined to May, nor to music; co[n]certs, classical and contempora[ry] dance performances and opera are [a]now included and the events la[st] through May and June and into Ju[ly].

Details from Teatro Communal[e,] Via Solferino 15, tel: 277 9236.

As Maggio Musicale tails out, t[he] **Estate Fiesolana** (Fiesole Summe[r]) arts festival picks up the baton wi[th] music, drama and film from the e[nd] of June to the end of August. M[ost] of the events take place in the Teat[ro] Romana (Roman Theatre) in Fieso[le] and at the Badia Fiesolana. Deta[ils] from the tourist information office [in] Piazza Mino, Fiesole, tel: 598720.

First Sunday after Ascension Da[y] the **Festa del Grillo** (Cricket Fes[ti]val) can be seen as a religious festiv[al] or it can be seen as a celebration [of] the joys of spring. Cascine Park, [to] the west of the city centre, fills wi[th] stalls selling crickets which are th[en] released to ensure good luck.

Calcio in Costume: literally tran[s]lated, this means 'Football in Co[s]

78

Fireworks in Piazzale Michelangelo

the Baptist, the patron saint of Florence; celebrations go on all night and there is a big firework display over the city, beginning at 10pm. Get a place on the north bank of the Arno for the best view of the fireworks.

AUGUST – DECEMBER

Festa della Rificolona (Lantern Festival): this is a much more low-key, but enchanting, festival which takes place on September 7, the eve of the Birth of the Virgin. Children process from all parts of the city to congregate in Piazza della Santissima Annunziata carrying paper lanterns on sticks, containing lighted candles.

During October and December: look out again for chamber concerts at the Teatro Pergola organised by the Amici della Musica. Concerts are also given in winter by the Orchestra Regionale Toscana in the church of Santo Stefano al Ponte and by other musical groups in many of the city's churches. The main opera season is October to March, with performances at the Teatro Comunale, Corso Italia 16, and the Palazzo Vecchio.

ame' and it is played on June 19, 24 nd 28, usually in Piazza Santa Croce ut check – sometimes it is held in iazza della Signoria and sometimes the Boboli Gardens).

The game is played by four teams, epresenting the four original *rioni*, r districts, of the city. The game is a ross between football and rugby. ut there are few observable rules, ne rivalry is intense and the teams metimes employ vicious tactics.

Each match is accompanied by a agnificent costumed procession. The ame held on June 24 is the most pectacular because it coincides with lidsummer and the Feast of St John

alcio in Costume, Piazza Santa Croce

GETTING THERE

By Air

The cheapest way to get to Florence is to fly to Pisa's Galileo Galilei Airport and take the train. Plenty of airlines offer scheduled and charter flights to Pisa but advance reservations are essential in the summer. The airport is pleasantly informal, yet efficient, and has exchange, car rental, shopping and duty-free facilities. For airport information, tel: (050) 28088.

Train tickets are bought at the kiosk to the left of the customs exit and Pisa Aeroporta railway station is located immediately to the left of the airport exit doors. Trains leave at least once every hour for Florence and the journey takes an hour.

Some airlines now fly direct to Florence Peretola airport 2 miles (4km) northwest of the city centre), though these flights tend to be more expensive. You can also fly to Peretola from Milan, Rome and Venice using Italy's domestic airline, ATI. Airport information, tel: 373498.

By Rail

The main railway station in Florence Santa Maria Novella, is served by fast intercity and sleeper connections from all over Europe, including the Italia Express from Strasbourg and the Palatino service from Paris. Ask your local travel agent for details; reservations are essential and the cost (depending on the distance travelled) may be greater than a charter flight unless you hold a rail pass that qualifies you for reduced fares. Information in Florence, tel: 278785.

By Road

If you can bear the long, uncomfor

ble journey, there are plenty of coach services to Florence from other European capitals. Again, you may find that flying is almost as cheap. Traveling by car is not recommended if only because you will have problems once you arrive; traffic is banned from the historic centre and parking is very difficult (the only car-park of any size is in the Fortezza da Basso, northeast of the city centre, behind the railway station). If you do drive to Florence, your best bet for a worry-free holiday is to find a hotel with its own secure parking.

TRAVEL ESSENTIALS

When to Visit

Although Florence is an all-year-round destination, the heat and crowds of July and August are best avoided; the crowds and queues can also be unbearable at Easter. Whenever you come, try to avoid Sunday afternoon and Monday when most museums, shops and restaurants are closed. May is probably the best month in which to see the city at its best, but June, September and October are also relatively cool and peaceful. November to March can be wetter and colder than you would believe possible in a Mediterranean climate but, to compensate, the city will be far less crowded and you will probably find bargain price air fares and hotel rooms. If you want to visit Florence during the Calcio in Costume festival you would be wise to book at least six months ahead.

Visas and Passports

Visitors from the US, EC and Commonwealth countries need only an up-to-date passport to enter Italy. Other nationals should apply for a visa in advance from the Italian embassy in their home country.

Vaccinations

None is required.

Customs

Items intended for your personal use can be imported duty-free and there are no limitations on the import of currency. EC residents aged 17 years or over can import the following duty-free (non EC residents have the same limits, except that the tobacco allowance is doubled; higher limits apply to goods purchased duty and tax paid within the EC):

Tobacco: 200 cigarettes or 100 cigarellos or 50 cigars or 250 grammes of tobacco.

Alcohol: 1 litre of spirits or 2 litres of still, sparkling or fortified wine.

Toiletries: 60 grammes of perfume or 250cc of toilet water.

Weather and Clothing

Winter in Florence can be bitingly cold but is often clear and sunny, so the city looks marvellous, although you will need an overcoat, gloves and hat to enjoy it. Winter can last until Easter and the short spring is often marked by heavy rain. Thereafter temperatures rise rapidly to 25°C (78°F) or more for the months of May to September. Florentines judge people very much on the basis of personal appearance so dress well, in smart casual clothes, rather than slumming it in untidy shorts, T-shirts and trainers. September to November are the wettest months, when a raincoat is indispensable.

What to Bring

Binoculars are a vital item of equipment if you want to study frescos in detail, since many of them are located high up on church walls. Real fresco freaks also bring their own illumination in the form of a torch with a powerful spotlight beam.

Electricity

The supply is 220 volts and the plugs are standard mainland Europe type, with two round pins. You will need an adaptor to use British three-pin appliances and a transformer if the appliances normally operate at 100-120 volts (eg, US and Canadian standard).

Time

Italy observes Central European Time (one hour ahead of Greenwich Mean Time) from October to April. Italian clocks then go forward by an hou in common with much of Europe.

Currency

The Italian *lira* (plural *lire*) is usual abbreviated to L or £. The lira now a relatively stable currency, b this has not been true in the pa when inflation was rampant – her you must get used to prices in t hundreds of thousands of lire (1 m lion lire is worth around £450 US$760, less than the average vi tor's budget for a week). Many Ita ians would like the government simplify the currency by knocking three noughts (ie, 1,000 lire wou become 1 lira), but so far this me sure has been defeated every time comes to a parliamentary vote.

Notes come in denominations 1,000, 2,000, 5,000, 10,000, 50,0 and 100,000 lire; coins in denomin tions of 50, 100, 200 and 500 li Telephone tokens (*gettoni*) are al accepted as coinage: their curre value is 200 lire. Coins and sm notes are no longer in short supp and you should not have difficu getting change for a 50,000-lire n – but it is worth keeping a supply 1,000-lire notes for small purchas such as a cup of coffee, a postcard museum admission fees. You will a need a supply of 100- and 200-l coins to feed into the electricity r ters in churches so that you can il minate the frescos.

Credit Cards

The major credit cards (Visa, Mast card/Access, American Express a Diners Club) are accepted in ma hotels, restaurants and upmar shops (look for a sign saying *Carta* – 'Card Yes' – in the window).

Taxis by the Duomo

30,000 lire. Traveller's cheques are also easy to exchange, but remember to present your passport.

Banks offer the best rates and are normally open Monday to Friday from 8.20am to 1.20pm. Some banks also open in the afternoon from 2.30pm to 3.45pm. The Banco Nazionale at the railway station is open continuously from 8.20am to 7.20pm Monday to Saturday. Outside these houses and at weekends you can always use automatic exchange machines.

Cash Machines

You can obtain lire from cash machines displaying a blue and red EC sign if your credit card displays the same symbol. You will need to key in the correct PIN number (check with your bank or card company before you go if you have forgotten your PIN number). The system is not infallible and if the machine swallows your card, you can usually retrieve it by presenting your passport to the bank within three days. This is an expensive way of gaining money, since you pay a handling charge of around 5 per cent and interest is charged at a very high rate from the moment you obtain the cash; it could, however, be useful in an emergency.

Several banks in Florence also have automatic exchange machines into which you can feed bank notes (those of the major European currencies or US dollars) and receive lire in return. Instructions are given in several languages and the exchange rate is the same as that offered by banks; the machines are, though, apt to reject notes that are creased or damaged.

Exchange

Eurocheques are widely accepted and are as good as money: each cheque can be cashed at a bank for up to

Tipping

Tips are not expected, but they are appreciated. Service charge is included in most restaurant bills but you may wish to leave a little extra for good service. 1,000 lire is an adequate tip for taxi drivers and porters.

USEFUL INFORMATION

Geography, Economy and Politics

Florence is the capital of Tuscany and lies on the Arno river, 50 miles/80km inland from the sea. The Arno valley and the plain to the west of Florence are heavily built up and industrialised; glass-making, motorcycle manufacture, textiles and goldworking are among the major industries, as well as intensive horticulture and market-gardening.

Florence itself is a major centre for artisan-based industries, such as *haute couture*, textile manufacture, leatherworking and paper-making; it also has a thriving service sector, which includes banking, legal services and insurance.

Florence is very much a busy working town, and this creates conflicts between the needs of residents and the demands made upon the city by the millions of visitors. Political debate centres round the issue of whether

an emergency, tel: 212222 for an am
bulance. The number for the hear
attack first aid unit is tel: 21444
Every public hospital in Florenc
has a casualty department (Pront
Soccorso) where treatment is fre
The most central in Florence :
the Ospedale Santa Maria Nuov:
Piazza Santa Maria Nuova, te
27581. Otherwise, medical care has
be paid for. EC nationals shou
obtain form E111 from po:
offices or health and social sec
rity departments in advance of the
visit and follow the instructions
obtain a reimbursement of the cos
Others should take out travel insu
ance providing cover for emergen
medical care.

Crime

Florence is a relatively safe city b
you still need to take sensible preca
tions to avoid pickpocketing or the
Keep photocopies of important doc
ments separately from the origina
to help the replacement process
they are lost or stolen. If you need
report a theft, go to the police st
tion (*questura*) on Via Zara 2 (t
49771) and make a statement (*denu
cia*) using an official multi-lingu
form, keeping one stamped copy
yourself as evidence for making an
surance claim.

The *Vigili Urbani* are traffic pol
whose main job is to prevent i
fringement of parking regulatio
and keep unauthorised vehicles out
the city centre during prohibit
hours. Local police matters are ha
dled by the *Polizia Urbani*. If y
need their help in an emergency, d
113. You may also see armed police
the *Carabinieri*; they are a natio
police force, technically a branch
the army, whose role is the handli
of serious crime.

or not business activities should be
relocated to a new satellite town, to
be built between Florence and Prato,
leaving the historic centre to tourism.
Many Florentines are strongly opposed to this proposal since Florence
itself is an inspiration to their cre-
ativity. Neither do they want Florence to lose its vitality and become a
'museum city' in which nobody lives.

HEALTH & EMERGENCIES

Pharmacies

A *farmacia* is identified by a sign displaying a red cross within a white
circle. The shops are staffed by trained
pharmacists who can prescribe drugs,
including antibiotics, that are only
available by doctor's prescription in
other countries. Normal opening
hours are 9am–1pm and 4pm–7pm
Monday to Friday. The address of the
nearest *farmacia* on emergency duty
will be posted in the window. The
Farmacia Comunale, at the railway
station, is open all night.

Medical Services

Call the Tourist Medical Service, tel:
475411, for advice. The service is
available 24 hours and a doctor will
visit you in your hotel if necessary. In

Toilets

Some museums have public toilets but elsewhere they scarcely exist. Toilets in bars are for customer use, so buy a coffee first and ask for the *bagno, toilette* or *gabinetto*. One toilet may serve for both sexes; otherwise they may be marked *signore* or *donne* for women and *signori* or *uomini* for men.

GETTING AROUND

Florence is so compact that you really can walk everywhere. You may, however, want to take the occasional taxi if you are carrying luggage or are out late at night. There are taxi ranks at the railway station and in most main streets and piazzas. For a radio taxi, tel: 4390 or 4798.

Buses

Buses in Florence are bright orange in colour and are run by ATAF. To save time trying to work out all the routes, simply remember that most buses pass through, and can be caught from, Piazza del Duomo or Santa Maria Novella station. Bus numbers and routes are clearly displayed at each bus-stop. Tickets are not available on the bus and must be bought in advance from bars and tobacco shops displaying the ATAF sticker. You will also find ticket-dispensing machines in the street alongside main bus-stops. The ticket should be fed into the stamping machine at the rear of the bus on entry. Each ticket is valid for 60 minutes' travel, during which time you can change from one bus to another as often as you need.

Maps and Guides

The most detailed map of Florence is published by LAC (Litografia Artistica Cartografica) and is called *Firenze: Pianta della Citta*. Of guides currently available, *Insight Cityguide: Florence* (Apa Publications) is the best for getting beneath the skin of the Florentines, whilst the Agostini guide to *Florence* (Istituto Geografico de Agostini, 1987) is the best for a comprehensive guide to monuments. Most museums in Florence now also sell excellent illustrated guides to their own collections. The travel bookshop called Libreria Viaggio, Via Ghibellina 117r, stocks a very good range of maps and guides to Florence and the rest of the world.

Tourist Offices

The main office is at Via Manzoni 16 (Tel: 247 8141) but this is a long way out of the city centre and is only open to the public in the mornings (9am–1pm, closed Sunday). Much more useful are the two branch offices in the centre. One is located in an alley south of Piazza della Signoria (Chiasso Baroncelli 17) while the other is next to the Medici-Riccardi Palace (Via Cavour 1r). Both are open to personal callers only (no telephone service) and are usually open daily 9am–7pm. Remember, too, that your hotel concierge will probably prove as knowledgeable and helpful as tourist office staff.

Hotels

Hotels in Florence are graded and priced according to their facilities. Cheap accommodation (1- or 2-star) does exist, especially in the area around the railway station, but most hotels in Florence are in the 3-star category or above – quite expensive, in other words, but you do get to stay in historic buildings, often of considerable grandeur and atmosphere. If you want a room in any of the hotels recommended below it is best to book in advance, especially for the Christmas, Easter and summer holiday periods. There is a room-booking agency at the railway station, open 9am to 8.30pm, whose services are available only to personal callers.

Price categories (for a double room): $ = 85-135,000 lire, $$ = 135-200,000 lire and $$$ = 200,000 lire.

ALBA
Via della Scala 22
Tel: 282610
Comfort at reasonable prices. Private parking. *$*

ANNELANA
Via Romana 34
Tel: 222402/3
Antique-furnished rooms in a gracious 15th-century former convent, built as a refuge for the widows of the Florentine nobility. *$*

APRILE
Via della Scala 6
Tel: 216237
Appealing hotel with a range of rooms to suit most pockets. *$*

BERNINI PALACE
Piazza San Firenze 29
Tel: 288621
Upmarket hotel with frescoed dining room and views of the Palazzo Vecchio. *$$*

BRUNELLESCHI
Piazza Santa Elisabeta 3
Tel: 562068
Located in a tiny central piazza and partly housed in a church with a 6th century tower. *$$*

CALZAIUOLI
Via del Calzaiuoli 6
Tel: 212456
Very central hotel in a 19th-century palazzo. *$*

CAVOUR
Via del Proconsolo 3
Tel: 282461
Recently modernised luxury hotel in the 14th-century Palazzo Strozzi-Ridolfi. Quiet location and fine views from the intimate roof-garden. *$*

CROCE DI MALTA
Via della Scala 7
Tel: 218351
Intimate hotel in a former convent with pool, garden and well-regarded restaurant. Private parking. *$$*

LE DUE FONTANE
Piazza Santissima Annunziata 14
Tel: 280086
Small modern hotel located on a quiet
and characterful square. Private parking. $

EXCELSIOR
Piazza Ognissanti 3
Tel: 264201
Old-world grandeur combined with
all modern conveniences; polished
service, luxurious rooms and fine Arno
views from the roof-garden. Private
parking. $$$

FERRETTI
Via delle Belle Donne 17
Tel: 261328
Cheap but clean and comfortable *pensione* near the station, favoured by
impoverished art students, writers
and photographers and run by
friendly Anglophile owners. $

GRAND
Piazza Ognissanti 1
Tel: 288781
Rival to the Excelsior in terms of *fin-
e-siècle* grandeur. Newly refurbished.
$$

HELVETIA & BRISTOL
Via dei Pescioni 2
Tel: 287814
Very central grand hotel, newly re-
furbished and full of antiques. Pri-
vate parking. $$$

JENNINGS RICCIOLI
Corso Tintori 7
Tel: 244751/2
Famous as the setting for E M
Forster's *A Room with a View* (Room
I, with its distant view of San Mini-
ato al Monte). Recently restored. Pri-
vate parking. $

HERMITAGE
Vicolo Marzio 1, Piazza del Pesce
Tel: 287216
Very central with views of the Ponte
Vecchio, although you may prefer the
quieter, viewless rooms at the back. $

LOGGIÀTA DEI SERVITI
Piazza Santissima Annunziata 3
Tel: 289592
Arguably the most characterful small
hotel in Florence, recently garlanded
with awards; set in a 16th-century
convent on the quiet piazza opposite
Innocenti, every room furnished with
antiques. Good value. $

LUNGARNO
Borgo San Jacopo 14
Tel: 264211
Modern hotel, very popular for its
views of the Ponte Vecchio from the
front rooms. Private parking. $$

MINERVA
Piazza Santa Maria Novella 16
Tel: 284555
Elegant hotel with fine views from
the rooftop pool and a garden restau-
rant. Private parking. $$

MONNA LISA
Borgo Pinti 27
Tel: 247 9751
Small but characterful hotel in a
14th-century palazzo, furnished with
paintings and antiques. The quieter
rooms, overlooking the delightful
courtyard garden, are the best. $$

PITTI PALACE
Via Barbadori 2
Tel: 282257
Small, traditional hotel just south of
the Ponte Vecchio, popular with English-speaking visitors because the co-
owner is American. Private parking.
$

PATRIZIA
Via Montebello 7
Tel: 282314
Good value. *$*

QUISISANA E PONTEVECCHIO
Lungarno Archiburieri 4
Tel: 216692
Used as the location for James Ivory's film of Forster's novel, *A Room with a View*; chosen, naturally, because some rooms enjoy sweeping views of the Arno and the city. *$*

REGENCY
Piazza Massiomo d'Azeglio 3
Tel: 245247
Grand hotel in a 19th-century palazzo with a highly regarded restaurant and elegant garden. Private parking. *$$$*

TORNABUONI BEACCI
Via de'Tornabuoni 3
Tel: 212645
Set in a 14th-century palazzo with roof-garden in the city's most prestigious shopping street. Private parking. *$*

VILLA CORA
Viale Machiavelli 4
Tel: 229 8451
Nineteenth-century villa in a rela-

tively rural setting with extensiv gardens, private parking, pool an good restaurant. *$$$*

VILLA SAN MICHELE
Via Doccia 4, Fiesole
Tel: 59451
The most luxurious of the city's grar luxe hotels, located in a former Fra ciscan monastery, partly designed Michelangelo, in the hilltop town Fiesole, 4 miles/6km north of t city; renowned for its super panorama over the rooftops of Fl rence. *$$$*

SAVOY
Piazza della Repubblica 7
Tel: 283313
Grand, but if somewhat faded, *fin-d siècle* luxury in the heart of the ci *$$$*

HOURS & HOLIDAYS

Business Hours

Shops generally open during the we Tuesday to Saturday from 9am 1pm and from 4pm to 7pm. Ma are closed all day Monday or at lea for the morning. Flower and ca shops open in the morning on Su days and public holidays, but ve little else operates during these tim although bars remain open all da every day. Many businesses, includi restaurants, close for two weeks August, the traditional holiday mon in Italy.

Museums and Monuments

Specific information is given in t itinerary section of this book, but t opening hours are notoriously subj to change at short notice. Many h tels keep a list of the latest openi times, so check before you set o and remember that most museums closed on Monday.

Churches are usually open from am to noon and from 4pm to 7pm or dusk in winter). Visitors are not llowed to wander round the church when there is a service on.

Public Holidays

Most businesses are closed on the following national holidays:
January 1
January 6 (Epiphany)
Good Friday
Easter Monday
April 25 (Liberation Day)
May 1 (Labour Day)
August 15 (Assumption)
November 1 (All Saints)
December 8 (Immaculate Conception)
December 25 and 26

In addition, many businesses lose for the period June 23–28 when the city celebrates the feast of its patron saint, St John the Baptist. August is the official holiday month in Italy when some shops and restaurants, though by no means all, will be closed.

You will have no difficulty in buying the major European newspapers, although perhaps a day late. If you read Italian, *La Nazione,*

Firenze La Sera and *Firenze Spettacolo* all contain details of local entertainment and events. Cultural events are listed in two English-language listings magazine, available in

Sights that are open when everything else is closed

Sight	Open Sunday pm	Open Monday am	pm	Open over lunch	Closing day	Itinerary number
Duomo (cathedral)	Yes	Yes	Yes	Yes	None	*Day 1*
Cathedral dome	No	Yes	Yes	Yes	Sunday	*Day 1*
Giotto's campanile	Yes	Yes	Yes	Yes	None	*Day 1*
Palazzo Vecchio	No	Yes	Yes	Yes	Saturday	*Day 1*
Uffizi	No	No	No	Yes	Monday	*Day 1*
Boboli Gardens	Yes	No	No	Yes	Monday	*Day 3*
Forte Belvedere	Yes	Yes	Yes	Yes	None	*Day 3*
Brancacci Chapel	Yes	Yes	Yes	(except Sun)	Tuesday	*Day 3*
Santa Croce	Yes	Yes	Yes	No	None	*Option 1*
Innocenti	No	Yes	No	No	Wednesday	*Option 2*
Firenze com'era museum	No	Yes	No	No	Thursday	*Option 2*
Museo dell'Opera	No	Yes	Yes	Yes	Sunday	*Option 3*
Fiesole sights	Yes	Yes	Yes	Yes	None	*Option 6*
Medici villas	Yes	No	No	Yes	Monday	*Option 7*
Most churches	Yes	Yes	Yes	No	None	

hotels or from tourist information centres, called *Florence Today* and *Florence Concierge Information*.

POST & TELECOMMUNICATIONS

Many bars and tobacconists sell postage stamps for letters and postcards: look for a sign with the white letter T on a blue background. For other transactions go to the central post office (Palazzo delle Poste) at Via Pelliceria 160, near Piazza della Repubblica, open Monday to Friday, 8.15am to 7pm and Saturday until noon.

Coin-operated phones accept 100-, 200- and 500-lire coins and can be found in many streets and squares; you can also phone from a bar if it displays a sign consisting of a red telephone handset in a red circle. Insert the coins before you dial and insert more if you hear a beep while you are still speaking; unused coins will be refunded after your call by pushing the return button. Many public phones also accept phone cards (*carta telefonica*), costing 5,000 lire, which can be bought in many tobacconists.

Telephone booths for long-distance or overseas calls are located in the central post office (open 24 hours, Via Pelliceria 160) and the railw station (open 8am to 9.45pm Mond to Saturday). Here you can make m tered calls and pay by cash or cre card. To get an international li dial 00.

To dial a local number, omit t area code; otherwise you need to d the city or district code, then t subscriber number. The engaged to consists of a series of rapid pips; t dialling tone is a series of long notes. When Italians answer the pho they invariably say *pronto* (meani 'ready').

The area code for Florence is 05 confusingly, telephone numbers in t city can have 4, 5, 6 or 7 digits.

FACILITIES FOR THE DISABLED

Nearly all the museums in Floren have wheelchair ramps and lifts. useful publication *Access to Floren* can be obtained from Mrs V Sau ders, Project Phoenix Trust, 6 Rochfords, Coffee Hall, Milt Keynes, MK6 5DJ.

FURTHER READING

f the many good books written bout Florence, Mary McCarthy's *he Stones of Florence and Venice Observed* (Penguin) remains the most imulating, but it assumes that you ready have a considerable knowlge of the city. As basic primers try R Hale's *Florence and the Medici* (Thames and Hudson) or Christopher ibbert's *The Rise and Fall of the ouse of Medici* (Penguin).

USEFUL ADDRESSES

irlines

IR FRANCE
orgo SS Apostoli 9
l: 055-218335

ITALIA
ungarno Acciaioli 10-12r
l: 055-27888

RITISH AIRWAYS
ia Vigna Nuova 36r
l: 055-218655

ERIA
azza Antinori 2
l: 055-215227

M ROYAL DUTCH AIRWAYS
azza Antinori 2
l: 055-284043

UFTHANSA
azza Antinori 2
l: 055-2381444

LYMPIC AIRWAYS
ia Por Santa Maria 4
l: 055-282338

S SCANDINAVIAN AIRLINES
ungarno Acciaioli 8
l: 055-2382701

SWISSAIR
Via Parione 1
Tel: 055-295055/6

TWA
Piazza Santa Trinita 1r
Tel: 055-2382795

Children and Youth Activities

The Cooperativa dei Ragazzi (Via San Gallo 27, Tel: 055-287500) has plenty of books (also in English and French) and games for children of all ages. The staff are also glad to pass on information. Sometimes there are performances in the afternoon.

LUDOTECA CENTRALE
(Piazza SS Annunziata 13)
Phone for information: 055-2478386.

BABY-SITTING
Via del Castellaccio 45r
Tel: 055-289382

Index

Art & Photo Credits

Photography **Robert Mort** *and*
Pages 8-9 **Albano Guatti**

Managing Editor **Andrew Eames**
Production Editor **Erich Meyer**
Cartography **Berndtson & Berndtson**

INSIGHT *pocket* GUIDES

• •

United States: **Houghton Mifflin Company, Boston MA 02108**
Tel: (800) 2253362 Fax: (800) 4589501

Canada: **Thomas Allen & Son, 390 Steelcase Road East**
Markham, Ontario L3R 1G2
Tel: (416) 4759126 Fax: (416) 4756747

Great Britain: **GeoCenter UK, Hampshire RG22 4BJ**
Tel: (256) 817987 Fax: (256) 817988

Worldwide: **Höfer Communications Singapore 2262**
Tel: (65) 8612755 Fax: (65) 8616438

❝ I was first drawn to the Insight Guides by the excellent "Nepal" volume. I can think of no book which so effectively captures the essence of a country. Out of these pages leaped the Nepal I know – the captivating charm of a people and their culture. I've since discovered and enjoyed the entire Insight Guide Series. Each volume deals with a country or city in the same sensitive depth, which is nowhere more evident than in the superb photography. **❞**

Sir Edmund Hillary

INSIGHT GUIDES

COLORSET NUMBERS

You'll find the colorset number on the spine of each Insight Guide.